Build Your Own Adobe

Kitchen area in the Aller adobe

BUILD YOUR OWN ADOBE

BY PAUL AND DORIS ALLER

STANFORD UNIVERSITY PRESS

STANFORD UNIVERSITY, CALIFORNIA

Stanford University Press, Stanford University, California

The Baker and Taylor Company, 55 Fifth Avenue, New York 3

Henry M. Snyder & Company, 440 Fourth Avenue, New York 16

Printed and Bound in the United States of America
by Stanford University Press

Dedicated to all the friends
and friendly relatives who
helped us build our house

Preface

BUILDING an adobe house is a whole lot easier than writing a book about how you did it. We know that, now that the house is finished and we are launched on the book. As Paul searches for the right word to describe what may be a simple procedure in the actual doing he moans, "I never expected to build this house *twice*." And it is building the house twice, this time on paper—retracing all the steps of construction from the test bricks through to the final details. If we were asked why we feel compelled to do it, we could only answer that it is because we feel obliged to tell others how they may have an adobe house by building it by themselves. In the telling we will stick close to our own experience, not because we believe that our way of doing a thing is the only way, or even the best way, but because it is backed by experience.

From our experience we say that you and your family can have that home in the country or the little house in the suburbs that you long for, if you have just half the gumption of your forefathers and will consider building with adobe and doing the work yourselves. You can have it even if you haven't much time, money, or building experience if you will use what leisure time you do have for the work and your money for materials, spending not one cent for labor, and if you will use your head to study each building problem as it comes up.

Using your heads and your hands and working with waterproofed adobe bricks as your building medium, here are some of the things you can do and the kind of a house you can have. You can make the bricks of almost any soil without intricate machinery or expensive ingredients, bricks that are "baked" by merely laying them out in the sun. With the waterproof bricks you can build walls that will stay dry in any climate. They will not sweat, nor will they crack in freezing temperatures since they take up no moisture, and they will not mold, rot, or rust. No rats, mice, or termites will nibble on them, nor will they burn. Adobe bricks make thick walls that need no added insulation to make a house that will stay warm in the winter and cool in the summer, walls that will effectively deaden sound and provide unusual accoustic properties, walls that need no special paints to preserve them, and walls that will last as near to forever as you need get. Best of all they are walls that you can build yourselves for they are made of small, easily made and handled units. An adobe house is one that you can be proud to own, but even more it is a house that is fun to build.

We had the time of our lives building our adobe. What we can't tell you for fear of sounding smug or sloppy is what working for ourselves has done for us, what it has done for our character development as individuals and our combined life as a family. When our offspring, Diane, missed the subject "Restoring the American Family" and spoke instead on "World Peace" at her recent graduation from high school, I was disappointed. Not that world peace isn't an important subject, but I would like to have heard her advising all the parents present that, if they would restore a sense of unity in the family, they should start building an adobe house at once with all the members of the family engaged in its construction on the theory that working together is a way to get along together. Just as well, perhaps, that she had another subject. A description of how the grown-ups and children alike can learn self-discipline and satisfaction in finishing a task begun might have sounded virtuous and dull unless she could have included some word pictures of the crazy fun and zany antics that went along with our construction job. She could have told of how three men, one on a step ladder, grunted and shouted "Hup, hup, hup!" as they pretended to be acrobats on a stage when they were really hoisting fifty-pound bricks to the top of a wall, while another man, clad only in shorts and horn-rimmed glasses, was doing an elaborate adagio dance with an adobe brick. But this would have sounded idiotic in a graduation speech!

It may sound so even here, but one way or another, we had so much fun building our adobe that we give you this blow-by-blow account and our blessing.

PAUL AND DORIS ALLER

Acknowledgments

WE WOULD like to say "thank-you" to our friends who have assisted us in the preparation of this book, particularly to Lawton R. Kennedy and James Fidiam for a number of the photographs.

We are also grateful to the Lane Publishing Company for permission to reproduce the frontispiece, originally used on the cover of the June 1943 issue of *Sunset Magazine,* and other photographs which have been previously published in *Sunset*.

Further acknowledgment of assistance is due to the *Woman's Home Companion* and to Gilbert Stanley Underwood, Supervising Architect, Public Buildings Administration, for their kind and gracious permission to quote from the excellent article "A Picnic to Build," written by Mr. Underwood and published in the March 1946 issue of the *Woman's Home Companion.*

Contents

Build Your Own Adobe

I

Building with Adobe

Mud, stuff that dreams are made of—doesn't sound right, does it? Yet, if a home of your own in the country is a part of your dream, it well may be that mud, common everyday dirt and water, may be the means of realizing that dream.

Although bricks made of earth and baked by the sun have been built into walls for centuries, adobe is just beginning to be recognized as a satisfactory, reliable building material for our times. The addition of a waterproofing agent to the same formula for making the ancient sun-dried bricks has added the quality of reliability which makes adobe a new idea for many home planners.

We made our private discovery of waterproofed adobe several years ago and have since built a week-end country house, a garage, and garden walls of it, making the bricks ourselves. To us, Paul and Doris Aller

3

and our daughter Diane, adobe means more than just a building material. It has meant hours of engrossing activity—an absorbing interest which has brought us new knowledge, new friends, new realizations of achievement. At present, adobe means this book which we hope will inspire homes for families whose incomes cannot keep pace with the increasing building costs of the standard, professionally built houses. We hope it will inspire houses for the many families now in rebellion against the sterile sameness of the standard house, because the use of adobe can give them homes with individuality. This old-new medium makes good houses with the full measure of shelter that a sheet-steel bungalow with a baked-on enamel finish can never give. Contempt for thin walls is the first mark of the adobe enthusiast and it is easy to see that we are enthusiastic about adobe.

A true adobe enthusiast can recite the virtues of adobe endlessly. He will have nothing but scorn for walls less than a foot thick, built to stand for centuries, and no good word at all for walls that shake when a door is slammed or walls that are vulnerable to tongues of flame, the sharp teeth of rodents, the hidden ways of termites, or the insidious inroads of rust and rot.

He can be equally eloquent on the artistic possibilities of the lowly mud brick, on texture and the play of light and shade on his favorite walls. On the other hand it is only fair to say that there are people who manage to remain indifferent to the whole subject of adobe. There are people who remain entirely unimpressed; they are convinced that building with adobe is but an adult game of mud pies, the safest course for the onlooker being to humor the players. One such, a casual observer of our bricklaying activities, caused us to look up from our work in horrified astonishment when he volunteered to tell us how we could make our beautiful walls "look just like stucco." This book is not for such as he but for the many persons who have expressed an interest in our house and have asked us so many questions about it.

We might say at this point that we don't pretend to know all the answers to all the questions that might be asked about adobe housebuilding. We have had the experience of making several thousand bricks and, although strictly amateurs, have built a very satisfactory country house without the help of professionals in any part. It isn't a big house nor are we particularly unusual people. In the same modest vein we can say that we never expected strangers to come for miles to see our house. But they do!

Why do people come to see this house that isn't big or imposing or really so different from many another house? It is a question we have often asked of ourselves. It may be because it is built of waterproofed adobe, not yet a common building material, but we can't believe that this is the only reason. We prefer to think that they come to see a house which they know to be the expression of one family, to be reassured that everyday people, perhaps they themselves, can still make a major and successful effort without the help of experts and specialists, without finance companies and time payments. We feel sure that it is the fact that we did all of the work of building with limited amounts of time and money, the money being on a strictly cash-as-we-went basis, that makes our house worth seeing or talking about or writing about.

It would be futile to deny that there was considerable work involved. There was a lot of hard and dirty work, but our friends helped us through the tough spots and our week-end labors were so mixed with kettles of stew and beans and cases of beer shared with congenial souls that none of us thought we were suffering any hardship. It may have been simple of us but we were under the impression that we were having a good time. Now when we are asked, "But wasn't it an awful lot of work?" we answer, "Yes, but it was a lot of fun too."

When we first got the urge to build a house we had an acre in Santa Cruz County and a well-established routine for leaving San Francisco on Friday nights to spend the week end in the country. On our acre we had a square board-and-batten house which stood, or rather rested lightly on scanty and decaying underpinnings. Without plumbing or electric wiring, it was the kind of a house that could have been built at any time since handy men first had access to sawn lumber and nails. The only running water in it came through the roof, and it was a damp welcome that the little shack gave us some Friday nights.

As a dwelling it was a poor thing, a shaky weakling with its short-comings concealed behind an immense climbing rose. That rose bush was something. Impressed by any show of strength and partial to things that are "hell-for-strong," we stood by admiringly while the green vines penetrated the roof, making more leaks of course, and we wondered how soon the tough shoots would come through the floor. Before that happened, however, the lusty growth of the rose wrenched the porch from the house and threw it to the ground. We were proud of our rose bush and ashamed for the house. Although it was as weathertight as a last year's bird nest, it did give us uncertain shelter while we planned and built our new house.

Besides the cracker-box house and the acre of ground, we had a car to take us from city to country. Paul had a steady job with a five-day work week and we were all in good health. Plus these things we had good friends and friendly relatives who liked to spend the week ends with us.

So much for what we had. Now for what we did not have. We didn't have any considerable amount of money earmarked for building or anything else. Payday was the important day of our week and still is. If any of us, including friends and relatives, had any special talents as builders none of us knew it at the time. Our knowledge of adobe, other than that Missions and other carefully preserved and historically important buildings were made of it, was nonexistent.

Shame on us for such ignorance! Not only were many of these Missions and historical monuments located in our own state, but only the year before we began house planning we had made a trip to Mexico where adobe is the prevalent building material. We had admired the Spanish-Colonial houses in Taxco, Mexico, but we really didn't study them until much later and then from a book found in the reference room of the San Francisco Public Library. (Garrison and Rustay, *Mexican Houses.*)

We'll have to confess that the charm of adobe wasn't fully appreciated until we heard of a method of making the bricks waterproof. It was a pamphlet published by the American Bitumuls Company in San Francisco (*Bitudobe for Modern Adobe Buildings*) that set us digging, not in the earth yet, but for further information. Every reference to adobe in the Public Library was pursued to its source. One of the most valuable references we had was a factual government bulletin, Farmer's Bulletin No. 1720, *Adobe or Sun-Dried Brick for Farm Buildings.* Another public service bulletin, *Adobe Construction in California,* No. 472, was obtained from the California Agricultural Experiment Station in Berkeley, California. Both of these bulletins are helpful, if unglamorously illustrated with pig pens and ugly bungalows. They could have been more depressing than inspiring but we didn't read them until our minds were made up.

Once settled on adobe we refused to be sidetracked; each of us was convinced that we were able both physically and financially to handle anything that could be done with single units. If we had to make each brick one at a time, we could; if we had to lay them in the wall one at a time, we could do that too. We never doubted that we would have some difficulties or make some mistakes and to help us over those we decided in the beginning to adopt an attitude we had seen displayed by the Mexican craftsman in Mexico.

It seemed to us that the Mexican worker, doing his job with materials which were plentiful and at hand and getting results unspoiled by factory-made perfection, had something we might well adopt. Whatever the material he did the best he could with it, and after doing his best he was content even if the finished product was a little crooked or lopsided. Built in the Mexican spirit, an adobe house takes kindly to a little crookedness here and there and bears a few bungles with serenity. We wouldn't have to be experts.

We quickly learned that there would be other advantages for the amateur doing his own work. Bricks could be made by hand or with a simple mud-mixing machine. The machine could be a secondhand plaster mixer, a dough mixer, or some homemade contrivance. The bricks could be made from almost any soil ("adobe" clay wasn't needed) and, particularly important because of our limited time, they could be laid into the wall at our own speed. No matter how slowly the work progressed, nothing would warp or rot or otherwise deteriorate. Also this absence of rot and decay in the finished building would be an asset since, even if it did take a great part of our young lives to finish, at least it would not be requiring a lot of our time on upkeep when we were old! As a matter of record, it took a surprisingly short time to lay the walls—two months from start to finish and that with a two-day work week.

It may be obvious to say that earthen walls do not burn; that no part of them is included in the diets of rats, mice, or termites; that they will not corrode or rot. Most listeners to a dissertation on the merits of adobe accept these facts without objection. They will also go along in agreement during discussion of the natural insulating properties of thick

Adobe may be mixed by hand (TOP) *or, with less effort, in a homemade mixer* (BOTTOM).

earth walls—walls that hold heat in and cold out in the winter and reverse the process in the summer. What some people will not accept readily is the statement that a house made of waterproof adobe will stay dry even in damp climates. They think earth attracts moisture and therefore an earth house must be damp. Actually waterproofed adobe bricks laid in the wall with mortar, likewise waterproofed with the same agent, make a wall that is drier than stone, building tile, concrete, common brick, or wood. Adobe walls do not weep, sweat, or absorb moisture.

What kind of house will you have? Adobe adapts to many styles. Traditionally it is suitable for the sprawling Western ranch house and the Pueblo Indian flat-roofed house common to the Southwest, but there is no reason why adobe should be so limited. Adobe brick can form the clean lines and planes of the modern-type house equally well.

Many charming houses of no set style or period use combinations of construction materials. Adobe is an excellent partner in these combinations. Sociable stuff, it mixes with and provides a harmonious foil for rough plaster, hand-hewn planks and beams, terra-cotta tile, concrete, and common brick, either new or used. If there are trees to spare on the property, poles and logs can be used in combination with the bricks to the advantage of both house and pocketbook. It might be safely said that adobe would go with whatever building material is at hand as long as it is a strong and durable natural material.

The same requisites, strength and durability, hold true for the furnishings and accessories for the interior of the adobe house. Furniture and decorative pieces will seem more appropriate if they are bold in texture and color. Handwoven textiles and rugs, bright copper and tin utensils, gaily patterned tiles, and handmade pottery move into an adobe and belong. Other arts and materials that live happily within adobe walls are richly carved wood and smooth or tooled leathers. In short any expression of man's art that is straightforward and sturdy will be welcome in the adobe house.

Would your family like living in an adobe house? Do you prefer a highly varnished surface on wood to a natural polish? Damask to rough-woven linen? Crystal to hand-blown bubble glass? Without condemning the more elegant items, it is likely that such taste would not be compatible with the crude roughness and weight of the adobe house. If on the other hand yours is the kind of family liking the things that

Adobe, redwood, wrought iron, and tile in pleasing combination.

show marks of their making and their makers, things with a last-forever quality, you will love the solidity of an adobe home.

We love ours. Now that the work on it is complete and it is an accomplished fact, no longer just an idea, we can say that we were not mistaken in our judgment of either our capabilities or our material.

In building we were handicapped by being eighty-six miles from our building site for five days of every week, but in a sense we turned that into an advantage by using the mid-week evenings to plan the coming week end's work. Even our social conversations were likely to turn to such subjects as plumbing, sewer systems, mud-mixing, electric wiring, and the like. So adept did we become at introducing these topics into any kind of conversation, it is a wonder that we did not alienate our friends. Instead most of them went right along with us and not only through the conversational phases, for they accompanied us on occasion to the country to take part in the current activity. They slept on hard beds and dined simply, since no one was willing to take much time out for cooking; they had no reward but our gratitude. The names of those who assisted us are carved on one of the big beams across the living room.

We are often asked about the cost of building with adobe and how much our own house cost to build. According to authorities an adobe house will cost approximately the same as a frame one of comparable size. Materials will be more expensive in the frame house and the labor cheaper. Labor is the expensive item in the adobe house and the materials cheaper. Obviously if the owner provides the labor he will pay only for materials. If part of these materials are secondhand, the cost can be reduced even further.

Concerning the cost of our house we are ignorant. The job of keeping the record was mine, and I failed miserably. After rounding up dozens of little notebooks I find they contain very little pertinent information, in fact most of the pages are still as blank as the day I bought them. The few notes and figures they do contain, such as "one small trowel, fifteen cents," simply will not add up to the total cost of our house.

To me, if not to the more budget-minded, the following things do add up: we were never in debt while building; we had and still have a very small savings for emergencies like an unexpected appendectomy;

we lived in the style to which we were accustomed and have continued to do so. In other words we are neither richer nor poorer in a financial sense. Of course it takes some money to build your own adobe house but there are other things equally important—the desire to own an adobe house, average muscular and mental development, imagination, self-confidence, an easy-going attitude and patience, and zeal and enthusiasm and friends who share it.

If you lack any of these but the first, which is absolutely necessary, you still need not give up the idea. They are likely to be acquired before the house is done and you will find the refreshing part of the whole undertaking to be that money, time, and specialized knowledge—all things on which so much stress is generally laid today—are not needed in any but small amounts at a time.

II

Making Bricks for the Adobe House

EARTH, water, and straw, with perhaps an additional dash of manure, were the only ingredients of the traditional adobe brick. The manure wasn't an essential; it was just a short cut to straw in convenient lengths —many a batch of modern adobes are made without straw at all since it adds little or nothing to the strength of the finished brick. When used it is because the straws act as "breather tubes" from the interior of the brick and allow for more even evaporation; also the inside of the brick can then dry at about the same rate as the outside, less checking and cracking resulting. Besides being made without manure or straw, modern adobes differ from their ancestors in another way, for although still largely made up of earth and water, they are made waterproof with asphalt emulsions.

13

The emulsified asphalt we used in making our bricks has the trade name "Bitudobe" and may be obtained from the American Bitumuls Company. Their executive offices are at 200 Bush Street in San Francisco. In our case the 55-gallon drums of emulsion were shipped from their plant in Oakland, California, but there are branches in various parts of the country and a near-by source could be found by writing to this company. Many large oil companies also sell these emulsions, or stabilizers as they are sometimes called. While we cannot quote prices, the cost per gallon is low and adds very little to the cost of the house while adding immeasurably to its value.

However, a test brick may be made without having any of the waterproofing agent at hand. These test bricks can tell you much concerning the suitability of your soil for making full-sized bricks, but before making even a single experimental brick it will be best to get an idea of the physical composition of your soil. To do this put a double handful of it in a glass jar or chemist's graduate and stir or shake it up. Allow it to stand a few minutes and you will see the muddy water clear as the suspended particles settle. The coarse sand will come to rest first on the bottom of the jar or graduate. The next layer will be made up of the finer sands and silts. The clay colloids, the finest of the soil particles, will remain in solution for several hours, but eventually they too will settle and form the top layer. This will be true whether the earth sample is taken from a mountaintop or the bottom of a swale, for soil is composed of these parts the world over. From this experiment it will be easy to see at a glance whether sand or clay predominates in your soil.

Were all the fine material in your soil sand, which is very unlikely unless you live on a desert waste, there wouldn't be anything to hold the sand together in a brick since it is the clay that acts as a binder. The clay parts of the soil are also the only parts that swell and slide in water, for sand is after all nothing but small pieces of rock and rocks don't melt and run in water. It is the asphalt coating around these minute pieces of clay that keeps them dry and prevents their sliding around. Hence the term "stabilizer" in referring to the asphalt emulsions. The amount of clay in proportion to sand must be known to determine how much stabilizer is needed.

Contrary to the ordinary conception, so-called "adobe" soil is not necessary in the making of adobe bricks. Not only unnecessary, it is positively undesirable since it is a very heavy clay and to be used at all would require the addition of quantities of sand. Many people ask us where we got our "adobe," meaning this heavy black clay. We had none, but our soil did contain enough clay to make incorporation of extra sand necessary. Fortunately it is often practical to use a blend of soils. Light soils will make good bricks by adding clayey earth and the clays will make equally good bricks when mixed with a few loads of sand.

To find out whether your most easily obtained soil can be used as is or if it needs to be blended with other earth, make a test brick. To begin it make a small mold of smooth boards approximately 2″ x 4″ x 2″ (inside measurements), open top and bottom; it might be called a box without bottom or lid. Take a sufficient amount of the soil to be tested to fill the mold and mix it with water to a mud-pie consistency. Wet the mold and set it on a board or other level place, then tamp it full of the mud. When the top has been leveled off, gently lift the mold away. If the mix was properly stiff the brick will not sag appreciably when the mold is lifted.

Let your sample brick dry several days. If you are impatient it may be dried out more speedily by putting it in a slow oven for a few hours. When it is dry, measure it to find how much smaller it is than it was before drying. If the shrinkage has been very great the chances are that it will show cracks, although there will be fewer cracks in a small brick than a full-sized one made of the same soil. Cracking, warping, and excessive shrinkage in drying are indications of too much clay in the soil for successful brickmaking.

After taking a good look at your brick, attempt to break it in your hands. You most likely can if you get a good grip on it, but if it requires some effort you may assume that properly made bricks of the same soil will be strong enough for the low walls of a house. If instead of resisting breakage the sample brick is crumbly and breaks with a mere twist of the wrist, it means that the mix was sandy and will make a weak brick unless a backbone of binding clay is added. How much pressure it takes to break an adobe brick can be measured scientifically by making compression tests. Specifications put out by the companies selling the asphalt stabilizers call for a brick which will resist breaking under pressure of from 300 to 500 pounds per square inch. The laboratories of these companies are equipped to make compression tests and can also be of service to you in testing your soil and estimating amounts of stabilizer needed. However, making your own test is valuable experience when you come to full-scale operations and should not be passed up.

We made our own tests and sample bricks and sent ten pounds of soil off to the laboratory as well. The most convenient way to send it was by Railway Express, and I shall never forget the bewildered look of the expressman in San Francisco as he bore it off. No wonder, for when he asked the value of my package I told him "No value." Making check marks on his records he asked next if it could be replaced. "Oh, yes," I replied, "I have a whole acre of it in Santa Cruz County." "Well, what *is* it?" the expressman persisted. I know he doubted my sanity when I convinced him it was only dirt, common everyday earth, but he carried it off.

It was true that we had an acre of the stuff as I had explained, but about half of our acre is hillside covered with eighty-year-old redwoods and other wild growth while the other half was at that time mostly under the old shack and taken up with fruit trees and berry vines. Besides the area set aside for the location of the new house, there was very little soil we could get to for purposes of brickmaking. This brings up an important point to consider in making your tests. Do you have a sufficient quantity of the tested soil to make the number of bricks you will need? We had to dig a deep hole (we called it our "adobe mine") to get raw material. If limited open space forces you to do the same, your test soil should be dug for too. A soil auger will do the trick and by boring into the earth you can also get a good idea as to what depth your soil remains uniform.

In estimating the amount of soil you will need, figure that a cubic foot of earth will make two bricks 4″ x 12″ x 18″. Bricks are often made other sizes but this is the size most commonly used. Since a brick this size weighs 48 to 50 pounds, it is easy to see that a larger one would be too heavy for easy handling. Furthermore a 12-inch wall can be laid single-brick thickness with a brick this size. It will take 173 of these bricks to make 100 square feet of wall when the bricks are laid to make a 12-inch thick wall.

If you plan a cellar under your adobe house, much of the brickmaking earth could be obtained from that excavation. The septic tank and tile disposal trenches of the sewage system require excavations that would provide extra soil for bricks or, if yours is to be a fancy estate, you might consider digging for a swimming pool first! We just dug a hole which we later filled with cans and garden refuse. A flower garden grows there now.

I doubt that adobe bricks have ever been made in more limited space than ours were. Although it is desirable to have plenty of space to lay bricks out for drying and curing, we didn't even have that. We stored them under the old shack and laid them out in rows between berry vines and in every odd corner. This made it necessary for us to use pallets made of laths and of a size to hold two bricks. With level ground to lay them out on, the pallets could be dispensed with and paper, burlap, or even a loose layer of sand might be used under the newly made bricks. In contrast to our tight working space, friends of ours who bought bare acreage with brickmaking in mind were able to hire a bulldozer and have huge piles of earth scraped up in very short order. This has its advantages over excavating although it makes a hot and dusty work site.

By now you should know something about the kind of soil you have and whether you have enough of it—two very important things to know if you plan to make your own adobe bricks. The next thing to find out is how much waterproofing is needed with your soil to make a good brick; the amount will depend on the number of clay particles. To determine this, build yourself a rough box 12″ x 12″ x 12″. Obviously this will hold a cubic foot and is as good a way to measure that amount of earth as any we know.

Put enough earth in the box to fill it when shaken down but not tamped in hard. Dump the earth, so measured, in a trough or metal wheelbarrow and dampen it with enough water to wet it through but not make it runny. When this is done add two quarts of emulsified asphalt and mix it with the mud until the whole mess is a uniform color. Make several of the small sample bricks as before and let them dry until hard.

When these specimens are dry, immerse them in a pail of clear, cold water for six hours or so. If the samples do not soften or discolor, the amount of stabilizer is correct. If the sample bricks take up water or soften appreciably, new ones should be made using up to three quarts of emulsion to a cubic foot of dry soil.

Old-time adobes were mixed by hand with hoes or by the feet of animals or humans. An area was spaded up and soaked and stable sweepings or other straw was strewn around liberally. Earth, water, and straw were worked together and in due time the whole mess was considered ready for scooping up and molding into bricks. Wetting the earth before mixing softens the clods and is a good practice, for it makes thorough mixing more certain, especially when the mixing is done by hand.

Although adobe can be mixed by hand it is a long, arduous task and one done better by machine. Machines suitable for mud-mixing are plaster mixers, dough mixers, or a homemade mixer such as ours was. Cement mixers won't do the work with mud.

We made our own mixer from a fifty-gallon oil drum, the gear-box from an ancient washing machine, a couple of pillow blocks, and a length of $1\frac{1}{4}$-inch reinforcing rod, heated and shaped around a junked automobile driveshaft, to make the mixing arms. This engineering marvel was powered by the two-horsepower gas engine that ordinarily pumped water from our well. Definitely a contraption, but it did the job and did it well.

Besides a mixer you will need sundry buckets and shovels, a convenient water supply, a barrel of stabilizer with spigot and stand, a deep wheelbarrow, and assorted brick molds.

The molds are constructed of 1-inch lumber surfaced on all sides, and for greatest strength the molds should be put together with screws. They are made double to mold two bricks at a time and are sometimes enlarged to turn out four bricks at a time, but it is a two-man job to handle these. Beside the regular 4″ x 12″ x 18″ bricks it is often a convenience to have some half this size, that is 4″ x 9″ x 12″, as well as a few 4″ x 6″ x 18″ to go around reinforcing rods; molds should also be made for these. The sizes given are for the finished, dry bricks. If the mud shrinks very much in the drying, molds should be made oversize to compensate. Allowance is usually a quarter-inch the 12-inch way, $\frac{3}{8}$ inch on the 18-inch side. The notched bricks for use around door and window openings are cast in the first two sizes given above by adding a 4-inch piece of 2″ x 4″ to the mold. A handle of some sort on the short ends of the mold is a help in lifting it.

If the brickmaking is to be a one- or two-man job it will go faster if quite a large quantity of mud is mixed and then dumped from the mixer into a large, flat trough and the molding done all at once. With a larger crew the mixing and molding can be going on simultaneously. Once under way, short cuts for your particular setup will present themselves. When we began we felt that 100 bricks a day was a fair output; before we had finished we were able, with four men working, to make 450 a day and this in our most unhandy location and digging all of our soil out of a hole in the ground. Altogether we made about 3,500 bricks for our house and garage and had a few left over for small garden walls here and there.

The work of molding the bricks will be easiest if the pile of previously wetted earth, the barrel of stabilizer, and your water supply are all close to the mixer or mixing box. The casting area should also be close at hand. A very few trial runs with the mixer will determine the ideal load. Measure the amount of soil put in the mixer by counting the shovelfuls it takes to make a load for your mixer. The earth must be measured so that the correct amount of stabilizer can be added. Procedure in mixing is to charge the mixer with the soil, add water, and mix thoroughly; then put in the proper amount of stabilizer. The straw, if any is used, can be added at any time. After the stabilizer is in, the whole is mixed until the batch is of a uniform color. A couple of test runs will work out the measure of water; only enough to make a stiff mix should be used because a soft mix will not stand when the molds are lifted. If an occasional soft mixture is turned out, it should be allowed to stand until it dries out enough to mold properly. The best and strongest bricks are made with a consistently stiff mud mixture, one which is plastic enough to handle with a garden spading fork.

With a batch of mud mixed the next step is to wet a mold and place it on a lath pallet, if the wet bricks are to be transported to the drying area, or else place it directly on the prepared surface of the casting place. Fill it with mud, tamping it firmly into the corners and at the edges with hands or a stick. Scrape the top level and remove the mold by lifting it straight up. Before the next bricks are molded the mold must be rinsed in water. A tub large enough to allow at least half of it to be immersed and a long-handled stiff brush make quick work of this rinsing.

Except where pallets are used, bricks are molded where they are to stay until dry enough to handle. In dry weather this is only a matter

The mold is filled (TOP) and smoothed off (LOWER LEFT). The mold is removed by lifting straight up, as shown in the illustration on page 13. Before the mold can be used again, it must be rinsed (LOWER RIGHT).

of three or four days. The bricks are then turned on edge and allowed to stand far enough apart for good air circulation between them. In a week or two they may be stacked. To save jockeying them around any more than necessary, it is a good idea to stack them in small piles close to the building site.

Rain will not hurt the bricks except in the first few hours after they are freshly made. Contrive temporary cover for them if it looks like rain while they are still wet. A cover to shield them from the direct sun may also be needed if your bricks show a tendency to crack while drying (cracking not due to lack of sand in the mix). This was our experience and we finally built light, movable short-legged shields of lath and paper to put over our new bricks.

If bricks continue to crack as they dry there are several possible reasons for it. It may be that more sand is needed, although too much sand will make a weak brick. To lessen evaporation cracks use as little mixing water as possible, avoiding sloppy mixes. The stiffest mud you can handle will make the strongest bricks too. If you haven't been using straw in your bricks and have trouble with cracking, add up to one-third of a pound of straw in short lengths to the cubic foot of soil. It is said that molding the bricks on a shallow bed of sand will lessen the friction as they shrink and minimize cracking. The addition of some sand and the portable covers were all that was necessary to reduce shrinkage and resulting cracks in our bricks.

The bricks are never piled flat for curing. Instead, stand them on edge in piles a few rows high to keep down breakage. One of the disadvantages of adobe bricks is their disinclination to travel well. They are heavy and awkward to transport. If they must be carried by truck they should stand on edge in the truck bed, and no more than one layer at a time can be hauled; this makes them quite expensive to transport for any but short hauls. Ideally, they are made and stacked quite close to the building site.

In the beginning of our adobe research we considered buying the bricks, but we soon abandoned that idea and as it turned out are quite glad we did. However, we can see how improvements could have been made in our brickmaking technique. If we were making bricks again and had at least a three-man crew and a location which permitted, we would like to do it a different way. We would have the mixer built up off the ground with a gravity feed for water and stabilizer, the soil disked and pushed up in a big pile behind the mixer. Then, with a low platform built in front of the mixer, the mud-mix could go directly into the mold on a pallet and the pallet with the bricks on it could be carried away and set on the ground. There the mold would be lifted, rinsed, and returned to the platform. In this manner production would be greatly increased.

A period of from thirty to ninety days should be allowed for the bricks to cure before they are set in the wall. How long the curing period should be will depend on the kind of drying weather, but ample time should be allowed, as "green" bricks will settle in the wall. If you are to be your own architect, however, you will not lack for things to do while your bricks lie in the sun. For one thing, you have some house planning to do . . . .

III

Planning the Adobe House

SOUND planning is the best way to begin most any endeavor, particularly building with adobe. If you know exactly the kind of a house you want and have it clearly pictured in your mind, that is all to the good, but having it in your mind is not enough, even if you do all the work yourself. Before any actual building is done, plans will have to be drawn and dimensions checked and double-checked. It is easy to make changes on paper, difficult on the building itself.

While making no claims for our abilities as draftsmen we did make working drawings for our house, using the conventional symbols and scales that are simple and easy to draw yet comprehensive. A book on architectural drawing for the beginner is good reading at this point, while a book of graphic standards for architects will provide a wealth of information.

To begin with we made preliminary drawings on ⅛-inch co-ordinate

23

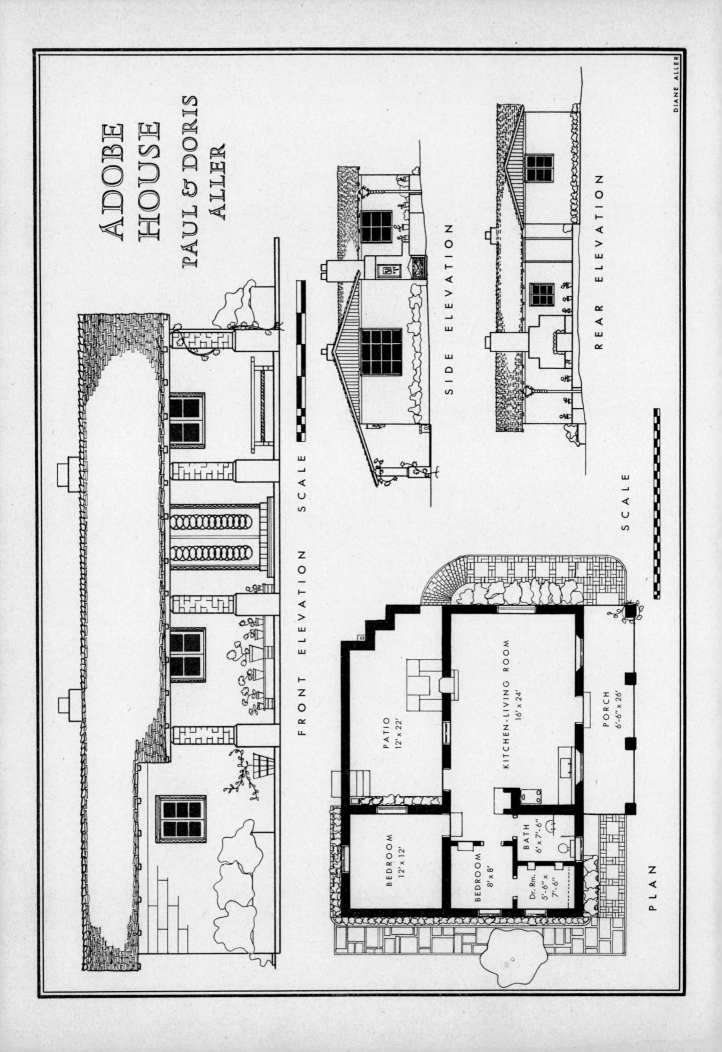

ADOBE HOUSE

PAUL & DORIS ALLER

FRONT ELEVATION   SCALE

SIDE ELEVATION

REAR ELEVATION   SCALE

DIANE ALLER

PLAN

BEDROOM
12' x 12'

BEDROOM
8' x 8'

Dr. Rm.
5'-6" x
7'-6"

BATH
6' x 7'-6"

PATIO
12' x 22'

KITCHEN-LIVING ROOM
16' x 24'

PORCH
6'-6" x 26'

paper (paper printed in ⅛-inch squares), placing the various rooms and checking measurements. After we had a plan that seemed to suit us we drew rough sketches of how the front, sides, and back of our house would look. These elevations were crude drawings, but we used our imaginations freely and they served to clarify our ideas. We also took into account the kind and amount of furniture we thought we would need for country living and placed it in scaled drawings on our tentative floor plan.

After we had developed the general plan of the house by means of these small-scale drawings and sketches, work was begun on a larger scale. Working drawings were made on tracing paper; the floor plan was developed first and then plans for the foundation, wiring, and roof framing were worked out on more tracing paper laid over the drawing of the floor plan. Of course we could not go far without working out the elevations showing the location of windows and doors, in fact the entire house must be considered as a whole in the planning stage. Thus the stove, the sink, refrigerator, and laundry equipment should be selected and dimensions known before the kitchen is planned. As for the bathroom, fixtures should be chosen or at least the dimensions known before that room is planned. How heat is to be supplied and what lighting fixtures will be needed and where they will be located must be thought out and noted on your drawings. All these things would be true in planning any type of house but are even more important in an adobe house. Amusing accounts have been written poking fun at the building trades describing electricians tearing out hunks of walls just built by the carpenters, of plumbers gleefully ripping out the plasterers' work and so on. It couldn't be done, even to make a funny story, in the building of an adobe. In ours, for instance, the conduit pipes which enclose the wiring to floor outlets were secured in place inside the foundation forms before the pouring. The floor drain for the shower and the sewer outlets went below the floor level and were placed there before the concrete slab floors were poured. It may be that there are other ways of doing these things, but whatever they are they must be planned for ahead of time and done in proper sequence because very few workers would tear into solid concrete just for fun. Moreover if you are the worker you'll want it right the first time. So in making your plans remember they are not just marks on paper but your actual house. Try to project yourself into the very rooms, walk in imagination around the outside, visualize how every part will look and how it will be built and go together. Build the whole structure on paper with your plans and sections, tearing them up and starting over as many times as you like; it will save time and trouble when building because chances are you will know them all by heart.

A good adobe house requires good planning in yet another direction. If you are to be your own architect you will need to know the restrictions inherent in the use of adobe. This building medium cannot be used in just the same way as wood or steel or concrete. All materials have limitations and adobe is no exception. Fortunately these limitations can turn into assets, since in the main they require that the general shape and design be kept *simple* and simple designs often make the soundest and most attractive houses. For example, amateurs are often afraid of their own judgment of proportion and line. In adobe masonry, wall height must be in definite mathematical proportion to the wall thickness; the length of a single unsupported wall is limited and openings in any single wall cannot exceed a certain percentage of solid unbroken wall. To our way of thinking these are protective features, practically insuring fine line and good proportion.

Other demands made on the material, such as thick lintels over doors and windows and buttresses to strengthen long walls, can be very decorative features. Again this is as we see it. However you look at them, as assets or limitations, they must be observed. Here are some of the rules as laid down in engineer's specifications for adobe:

The height of a wall (measured from the top of the foundation to the roof plate), 12 inches thick must not exceed 9 feet. A wall 13 inches thick, 10 feet; 14 inches thick, 11 feet; and 18 inches thick, 14 feet.

The maximum length for walls unsupported by buttresses or cross walls is 25 feet. Partition walls of brick are considered cross walls but frame ones are not. A buttress is an additional pillar of bricks incorporated in the wall.

Wall space between doors or windows should not be less than 3 feet. The minimum span between a corner and an opening is likewise 3 feet. Corner windows are not recommended for adobe structures.

Openings in the wall should be measured and totaled in square feet. This total should not exceed 40 per cent of the total square feet of wall.

This means that a little less than half the wall can be window or door space, not more.

Lintels and sills made either of timber or reinforced concrete, not less than 6 inches deep and full wall width, should run over and under all windows and doors; these should extend not less than 9 inches on either side of the opening.

The sides of all wall openings should be strengthened with steel reinforcing rods running vertically from the foundation to the bond beam at the top of the wall. From the foregoing you can see that the holes in an adobe structure are its weakest parts; therefore braces must go around and over any gaps in the wall.

The bond beam mentioned above is a 6-inch-deep, wall-width, concrete topping for the wall and is reinforced with steel rods. It runs continuously around the top of all adobe walls, interior and exterior. Where the walls are low, doors and windows can be planned to extend to the bottom of the bond beam, or collar beam as it is sometimes called, thus doing away with lintels over windows and doors. Most of the openings in our house are this way. Anchor bolts for the roof plate are set in the bond beam at the time it is poured. Irregularities in the height of the wall, and there are bound to be some, can be evened up with the concrete wall cap, which is also a means of strengthening the building.

Earthquakes are a real menace to masonry buildings in some localities, and this should be taken into serious account. So far our house has withstood several temblors, one severe enough to rout us all from our beds, without showing so much as a crack. Here in California we can expect the earth under our house to quiver and shake once in awhile, so we took every precaution to build it as a unit that it might continue to stand as one, come what may. To this end we used reinforcing steel rods in a heavy concrete foundation; more rods extend vertically along every wall opening, reaching from foundation to collar beam. At the bottom these rods tie to those in the foundation, and at the top they tie to those in the collar beam. Joined in this way the steel makes a light, invisible skeleton inside the walls. Further strength was gained by using concrete mortar throughout in the bricklaying. Double strands of barbed wire, held in place by large wire staples, run through the mortar between every sixth course of bricks and is fastened to the jambs alongside windows and doors. No breaks in the wire were allowed to occur at corners, and where it was necessary to make a splice the wire was overlapped for at least 18 inches.

Our neighbors, none of whom were engineers however, shook their heads over all this steel and wire and concrete and said that we were going to unnecessary lengths. The added expense was negligible and we thought it worth the extra work, knowing these same neighbors would shake their heads and say "I knew it!" if our house fell down.

Besides the methods described to minimize earthquake danger, further protection can be added by the general shape of the house. A square is the strongest, but your house needn't be square although basically it should be a rectangle or a series of rectangles placed to buttress one another. If properly planned, solid partition walls can serve to support long side walls. Long, thin wings or wings placed at an angle other than 90 degrees to the main body of the house are not desirable for adobe, particularly when planned by amateur engineers!

When we came to the place where we had to plan the roof, decide on the slope, the amount of overhang for the eaves and other kindred details, we found that a little cardboard model built to scale was of help. We "tried on" several kinds of roofs over these cardboard walls. In the end we decided on a gable roof with the lowest possible pitch for shakes. The gap between the top of the wall and the roof peak, known as the gable ends, we elected to fill in with frame construction and did not carry any adobe past the collar beam. It is possible to step the bricks up to fill in the triangular space, binding the edges with another concrete form, but it is easier to get boards and nails that high off the ground than it is to hoist bricks and concrete. Our vertical boards were easy to put up; we stained them a dark brown which looks very well with the white brick walls.

We simplified our building in other ways too. For example, to save money as well as work, we kept all the plumbing fixtures close together. Water pipes and vents were kept short by putting kitchen sink, storage tank for hot water, and the hot-water connections to the stove on one side of a partition. Directly opposite, on the other side of the same partition, we located washstand, shower, and toilet.

A look at the floor plans of the Aller adobe reveals that the living room, dining room, and kitchen are not separate rooms at all but are contained in one large room. Having the kitchen sink and stove in the living room may be an odd notion but we like it. No matter how small or large the kitchens have been in the different places we have called home, certain hours of the day would find the whole family and usually about six others jammed into the kitchen. Country house guests also show a preference for being in the kitchen at rush hours we found. More resolute cooks can invite their most-interested audience to leave while they prepare a meal, but as cook I still don't want to miss anything, so we naturally wanted a large kitchen. We also wanted a large living room and a place for a big dining table. Separate rooms for all these functions would add up to too much house, so we compromised on one large room to house them all and it works out most satisfactorily for week-end living.

If fireplaces interest you, plan to have a distinctive one, one in harmony with the rest of your room, one adapted to the way you will use it. Will the hearth be ornamental only or will you do some of the cooking on it? Will it be the focal point of the room or an accessory? Consider what you want in a fireplace besides a fire. Our fireplace has no mantel, for as a family we consider any cleared surface the logical place to unload our various personal belongings as we enter any room. Paul pleads with me to keep books, clothes, and other of my effects out of the chairs. He just might get time to sit down. I beg him to keep his things any place but on the mantel, smack in the middle of my carefully thought-out decorative arrangement. He doesn't, and in no time at all the mantel looks as though it were set up for a surrealistic painting. After a quick mental picture of the assortment that could find its way to a country house mantel, the whole problem was solved by dispensing with one altogether. We still have chairs, however.

Unlike most home planners, Paul wasn't seduced by the idea of an immense fireplace. Being a practical man, he thought of the amount of wood chopping and fuel carrying that a big fireplace calls for and said he wanted the tiniest of fireplaces. Diane pointed out that a little fireplace, placed at floor level where it would also be very much below eye level, was going to look more like a hole accidentally burned in the wall than a fireplace, particularly if there was to be no mantelpiece. As a result of these stipulations we built a small fireplace nearly waist high which puts a nice little fire where we can look at it and enjoy it without devoting our lives to fueling it. No matter what you decide you want of a fireplace in your adobe house, it will be built in the customary manner except that the bond beam which goes around the top of the walls will go around to take in the chimney if it is on an adobe wall. It may be faced with adobe brick, common brick, or field stones, as long as the adobes or field stones do not come in direct contact with the fire. Adobe will chip or crumble near intense heat, while field stones are never advised for use close to the fire since they may explode and send the rock chips flying if they get too hot; the best fireplace lining is still regular firebrick. Chimneys should be lined with tile flue lining. A combination outdoor fireplace and cooking grill is directly behind our little fireplace in the kitchen–living room. Both share the same chimney but each has a separate flue.

We were aided in the fundamental working designs of our fireplaces by the Farmers' Bulletins No. 1889, *Fireplaces and Chimneys,* and No. 1649, *Construction of Chimneys and Fireplaces.* (See chapter v, "Laying the Walls of the Adobe House," pp. 55–56.)

If your climate demands more heat in the house than can be provided by fireplaces, which are far from being the most efficient and cheapest means, decide how the heat is to be provided and what space the device will take and plan accordingly.

Light must be planned for as well as heat and again this is easiest done on paper. How many floor plugs and appliance outlets you will need and where they should be placed will have to be thought out. We set our floor plugs directly in the foundation with the wire enclosed in conduit pipe. The wiring to the wall switches goes through more conduit laid alongside the door jambs. The overhead wiring is concealed inside partitions where possible and for this we used non-metallic sheathed cable. (See chapter viii, "Electric Wiring in the Adobe House.")

Closets and storage spaces form a subject often neglected when most houses are planned or so it would seem from the numbers of howling housewives demanding bigger and better places to hide things from the male members of their families. I wanted a large walk-in closet and got it, but since then I have read that big closets are less efficient and waste more space than small ones if the latter are plentiful. I wouldn't know and from my own experience can only conclude that one woman's closet is another's catch-all since ours are all strictly Fibber McGee.

Having a place for everything is no guaranty that everything will be in its place in our house, but it may be in yours if you plan it that way. Farmers' Bulletin No. 1865, *Closets and Storage Spaces,* may help you; in it are plans for all kinds of cupboards, closets, and storage units.

Before your plans are complete be sure that you have checked them, not only for practical structural details, but with opportunities in mind for each member of the family to have some fun by expressing a talent or indulging in a pet hobby. If you have never painted a mural, for example, but have a desire to do so, reserve a good wall space to paint it on. It's your house—exercise your whims and fancies on it. In one way or another an adobe house can offer a background for every member of the family to display his or her talent to advantage of both house and family. Diane developed an interest in tile mosaic on seeing a mosaic artist at work at the World's Fair at San Francisco and her first effort in that direction adorns the floor of our shower. Since then she has designed and set mosaics in a bench which is built into the wall at the entrance of our place, and last summer she completed an aquatic design in tile to cover the bottom of a reflecting pool 5'- 9" x 8'- 3" in our garden. The wide window sills throughout our house are all tile-faced color arrangements, and the finished job of setting the tile was done by our daughter.

My woodcarving ornaments every surface suitable to this type of decoration; the painted decorative panels on the inside of the gable ends of the kitchen–living room are my work and so are most of the lighting fixtures. Furniture- and cabinet-making reflect Paul's special efforts.

Our house is ours by virtue of more than just owning it. To make your house yours in the fullest sense, encourage every member of the family to specialize on some part of its building or decoration. If some of them are quite young and unskilled, it is still possible to find things within their capabilities, and there is no better way for a family to learn co-operation and good will toward one another than working together. Naturally a certain degree of craftsmanship must be demanded, but if the result of childish or unskilled work is somewhat crude or primitive, the effect of it will be in keeping with a strong, unpretentious house.

There has been much written on house planning and you will surely read or have already read some of it. I have yet to talk houses with

This small fireplace with its raised hearth—we sometimes cook on it—is especially suitable in our kitchen–living room.

anyone who hasn't had or doesn't have a pet idea of his own on house-building. Yet, considering the wealth of information available on good houses and the original ideas of the average planner, houses seem for the most part very mediocre—impersonal shells for humans who, from the scope of arrangements ordinarily provided, are expected to do little but eat, sleep, and bathe. It has occurred to me to wonder if perhaps living in dull houses might not make dull people, people who really never do anything while at home but sleep, eat, and bathe? This may be just a flight of fancy on my part (I am given to them), but it isn't a mere fancy notion to consider what you want to do in a house and plan it accord-ingly. A country house is a good place to let yourself go and be different. Instead of counting off standardized room names: living room, kitchen, bedroom, and bath—why not say instead: a place to read, write, eat, sleep, play games, sew, paint, or whatever you must do and want to do? Let preconceived ideas go by while you plan a corner or a whole room for every activity. Juggle them around until you get a degree of privacy for those functions which call for it, suitable exposures, convenient traffic lanes, or whatever seems of prime importance to you. If you wind up with the kitchen stove in the living room as we did, let us assure you that that isn't an impossible arrangement by any means.

Books on home planning often warn against an unusual arrange-ment for fear some hypothetical future buyer might not like it. A "freak" house is said to be hard to sell and building and loan companies will not lend money on them. Nevertheless, nearly every seeker of a ready-made home sets out to find something different and unusual. Only after he fails to find it does he settle for the strictly conventional house. Friends of ours built an uncommon house expecting to stay in it forever but were finally forced to put it up for sale. When they first showed it to a real estate man they were apologetic about the unique features of their house. He comforted and amused them by saying, "Don't worry. I'll find some other squirrels who will like it." He did too, and squirrels or no, the new owners are entranced with it and our friends lost nothing by building and living in the kind of a house they wanted.

The house hasn't yet been built that would please every potential home owner. But in some book or magazine you may find a plan that comes very close to what you desire and you can adapt it to your ideas and building site. First consideration is usually given to the floor plan.

This is a good approach since a house must, first of all, provide proper space for all family activities. Don't start with a set notion concerning some exterior type or style that you think you must have and try to force the interior arrangement to fit it, as a pleasing outside form will usually result if the interior is truly functional.

If there are building codes in effect where you intend to build, it would be well to know them when you are still just drawing plans. These codes are concerned with community safety more than with personal living arrangements. Sort your ideas on houses and discard those based only on habit or custom and have a house that will be fun to build, fun to own, and above all fun to live in.

IV

Foundation for the Adobe House

NOW that the bricks are made and the plans drawn, the time has come to think of the foundation for the adobe house. As the base of the whole structure it is a very important part.

The work of making the foundation falls under two headings: building the wooden forms and filling the forms with concrete. If you can enlist friends to help with the work on both phases it will speed the day you start bricklaying; you will need help especially when it is time to mix and pour the concrete. If you would benefit by our experience, invite only your nondrinking friends.

We overlooked the last point in the paragraph above; to be truthful, we gave it nary a thought, and as a consequence Paul composed the motto, "Let no man trifle with the foundations of another man's house," and we had one of the craziest Fourths we ever hope to live through. The long holiday seemed a perfect time to do the job of pouring the main part of our foundation, so we gathered our hardest-working friends about us. The holiday spirit took hold of our volunteer crew early and before long certain of them were boasting that they could mix better concrete while intoxicated than they could cold-sober. Others were rapidly losing even the power of speech, let alone co-ordinated action. The rumbling of the cement mixer, the gleeful shouts of the merry-makers as they threw shovels of sand and cement in its direction, the frequent toasts, and the desperate expression of Paul's face and mine must have combined in a scene to make the gods laugh. We weren't able to laugh until later when the day was saved by the departure of the celebrants and the arrival of sober help. With a fresh start we finished before dark but we didn't stay up to see the fireworks.

Enough of the revelry that inadvertently accompanied the pouring of our foundation and on to the serious side. We cannot cover all the problems common to foundations, but a description of our procedure should be of help. At the end of this chapter is a list of booklets which we found, containing specific information of real value.

As the earth under our building site was quite firm, footings were dispensed with. The ground does not freeze in our part of California, so no precautions on that score were needed either. If you are building in a part of the country where the ground does freeze, you will follow local custom as to foundation depth. Usually the building code of a near-by city will provide specifications for your locality.

If you have reason to doubt the bearing qualities of your ground you can do one of several things: make your foundation extra strong with wide footings poured first and the foundation proper set on top of that, make a special study of computing footing dimensions for certain conditions, etc., or as a last resort take your plans to an engineer and let him do the figuring. The weight of adobe walls is assumed to be 120 pounds per square foot.

If your house will not be located on firm ground, if it is to be on a steep hillside, or if you plan to have deep cellars, special foundations should be designed by someone familiar with structural mechanics. If you have none of these problems, however, you should be able to make your own foundation plans.

Once these plans are drawn, the next thing to do is to lay it out on the actual site. To do this, locate and measure the outside front line of the foundation with a steel tape; this will serve as a base line. Drive a stake at each end of it in such a way that measuring from the center of one stake to the center of the other will give you the exact length of the front of the house. Mark centers on the stakes with nails representing the two front corners. Stretch a line between them. Put a second string on each nail and run it back to represent the sides of the house. Fasten the ends of these to preliminary stakes, setting stakes and lines as accurately as you can with a carpenter's square. To square lines still more accurately, measure in from the ends of the front corners for a distance of 6 feet and mark it with stake and nail. Measure from the front corner along the sides for a distance of 8 feet and mark the same way. When the diagonal measurement from the 6-foot mark to the 8-foot mark is exactly 10 feet, the lines are squared. Shift the temporary back lines and stakes until you get a reading of 6′-8′-10′ on each corner. Measure the lines on the side and set stakes to mark the back corners and check for squareness as already described. To check still further, take criss-cross measurements. These diagonals should be the same. Accuracy here will save work and worry later.

With an irregularly shaped building it is advisable to first lay out a large rectangle embracing the entire building or the greater part of it. With this established, the remaining portions of the layout will consist of smaller rectangles, each of which may be laid out and proved separately.

About 4 feet from each corner, set the batter boards. (See drawing.) The top of the horizontal boards may be set level with some convenient datum point, usually the top of the foundation or at the floor level. Use a carpenter's or mason's level or a line level. Transfer the marking strings from the first stakes to the batter boards all around and check corners and diagonals once more.

As excavation trenches are usually about a foot wider than the actual foundation, excavation lines may be determined by measuring 1 foot out from the inner and outer foundation lines. When all lines are set and checked, make saw cuts about a quarter-inch deep where the strings cross the batter board so they may be easily put back, for they will need to be taken down frequently.

As our house is situated on a slight grade we planned it on two levels; thus there is a step up to the larger bedroom. This saved a lot of digging,

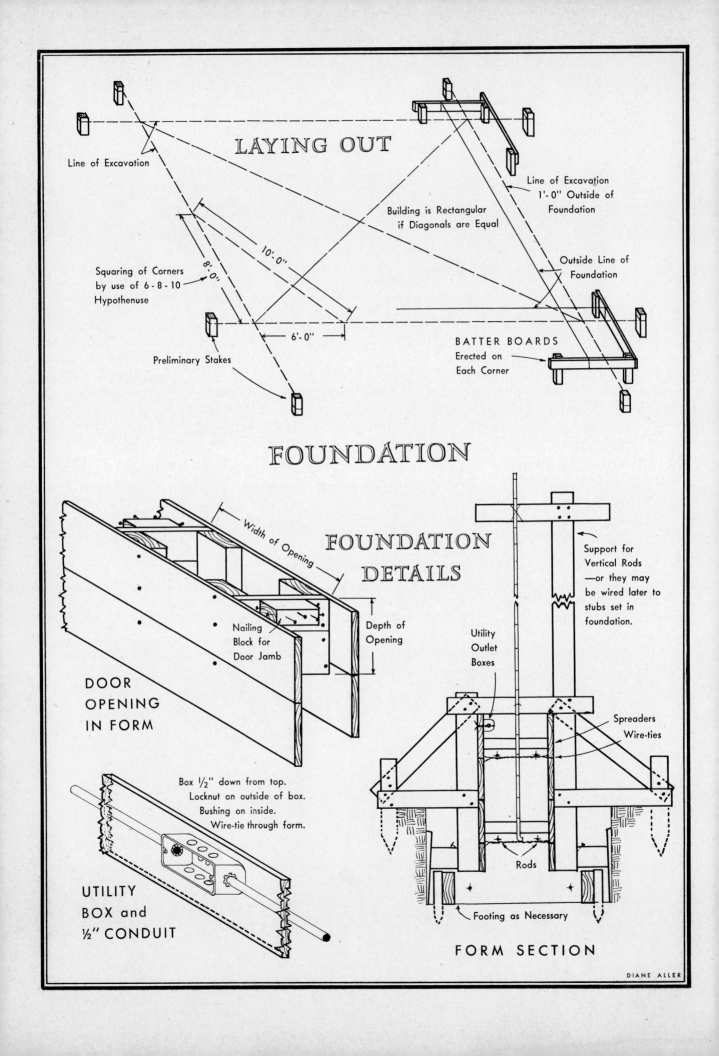

LAYING OUT

Line of Excavation

Line of Excavation
1'- 0'' Outside of
Foundation

Building is Rectangular
if Diagonals are Equal

Outside Line of
Foundation

10'-0''

Squaring of Corners
by use of 6 - 8 - 10
Hypothenuse

8'-0''

6'-0''

BATTER BOARDS
Erected on
Each Corner

Preliminary Stakes

FOUNDATION

FOUNDATION
DETAILS

Width of Opening

Depth of
Opening

Nailing
Block for
Door Jamb

DOOR
OPENING
IN FORM

Support for
Vertical Rods
—or they may
be wired later to
stubs set in
foundation.

Utility
Outlet
Boxes

Spreaders
Wire-ties

Rods

Box ½'' down from top.
Locknut on outside of box.
Bushing on inside.
Wire-tie through form.

UTILITY
BOX and
½'' CONDUIT

Footing as Necessary

FORM SECTION

DIANE ALLER

and that is what the next step of the foundation consists of mainly—a lot of digging and dirt moving.

Before you start to dig, scratch the earth with a pick or a spade along the excavation lines and then put the strings aside to keep them out of the way. There isn't much to be said for or about this phase of the work. Dig to the required depth and remove loose earth from the trench. Building the forms will be easier if the bottom of the trench is kept as smooth and level as possible. Needless to say, any pipe that goes under the foundation is installed while the trenches are open; they should be plugged to keep dirt or concrete from getting in them.

The foundation for adobe is always the same width as the wall is to be, so ours is a foot wide. It averages about 3 feet deep. We used 1″ x 8″ lumber for form walls, bracing them at 2-foot intervals. As wet concrete is very heavy, about 150 pounds per cubic foot, the pressure on the forms is considerable and construction should be strong and well-built. Braces on our form were two-by-fours. Along the sides of the windows and doors, 8-foot lengths of two-by-four extended upward to hold the vertical rods steady.

The outside wall of the form was built around the entire structure first. (The fireplace foundations were considered as part of the house foundation and poured at the same time.) This was leveled and squared before starting the inside form. At a low level, wire ties were run through the joints in the form boards and around the outside braces. Others were placed near the top level of the form. They were not drawn tight until spreaders (boards cut 1″ x 2″ x 12″) were placed inside the form to hold the two walls apart while the wire ties pulled them together. The wooden spreaders are removed as the concrete is poured, but the wires stay in and the loops over the braces are snipped to remove the forms.

The top of our foundation was planned to be 6 inches above the finished outside grade, the finished floor level 4 inches below the top of the foundation. This gave us a concrete "mopboard" inside and allowed space to install electric floor plugs. The sills of the door openings were sunk below the finished floor level.

As the top of the foundation was above the floor level it was necessary to block out door openings with cleats and partitions nailed to the form boards. (See drawing.) The opening was made deep enough to reach to the rough floor level which was 5½ inches below the top of the foundation, tile and mortar making up the 1½ inches to finished floor height. It is not necessary to put a bottom across between these stops, since concrete will not rise and fill the openings if reasonable pains are taken to see that it doesn't. Nailing-blocks for the lower end of the door jambs are provided by nailing blocks of wood 2″ x 4″ x 6″ to the backs of these partitions in the form. These nailing-blocks are sometimes referred to as "bucks." Nails driven part way in these and allowed to extend into the concrete will hold them firm when the form boards are stripped off.

An opening for the sewer-outlet pipe may be allowed for by building and installing a 6″ x 6″ open-ended box in position across the inside of the form. The boards can be knocked out when the concrete is hard and will leave an opening 6 inches square through the foundation. After the pipe is in place, any open space left can be chinked with mortar. Openings through the foundation for water pipe can be made by boring holes the proper size through the form and inserting short lengths of pipe. If they are greased before the concrete is poured they will be easy to remove.

Next to go inside the forms is the reinforcing rod. We used two half-inch bars around the bottom level of the form and two more on the upper level. They were supported by and fastened to the wire cross ties and were continuous around corners. Where a splice was necessary an 18-inch lap was allowed. All of the steel rod was fastened to hold it 3 inches in from an outside surface. After the horizontal rods were in place vertical ones were put in. Careful measurements were taken for window and door locations and the rods went up alongside them, fastened to the upright two-by-fours. The ends inside the foundation were bent to right angles to make a 2-foot leg which was tied with short lengths of wire to the horizontal rods in the form.

By this time the contents of the form are beginning to look complicated and just reading this may make you wonder if there is going to be any room left to put concrete! And there is still the conduit pipe to hold the wiring for the base outlets and the outlet boxes to put in. We used half-inch conduit and the "deep" type of utility box. The latter were held flush against the inside wall of the form by passing more wire through holes in the backs of the boxes and small holes drilled in the form boards. Stuffing the boxes with cotton wadding kept the concrete from leaking into them.

A useful tool for bending both the reinforcing rod and the conduit pipe is a 3- or 4-foot piece of 1-inch water pipe threaded at one end and a 1-inch T screwed on it.

With the forms complete, it is time to get ready for the actual concrete pouring. To determine the amounts of sand, gravel, and cement you will need to do the job, you must first measure the forms and compute the number of cubic yards they will hold. Where the foundation is 1 foot wide and of a uniform depth it is easy to figure the cubic feet; the total divided by 27 will give the answer in cubic yards.

Using the standard mixture of 1, 2¾, and 3 (1 part cement, 2¾ parts sand, 3 parts rock), it will take five sacks of cement, over half (.52) a cubic yard of sand, and roughly three-quarters (.74) of a cubic yard of coarse aggregate for every cubic yard of space to be filled. If you buy "concrete mix" (a combination of sand and rock in proportions of 2¾ parts sand to 3 parts rock) from a building-supply business, you must have approximately 1¼ (1.26) cubic yards of the mix and five sacks of cement to the cubic yard of space. Since the material compacts when mixed it takes 1¼ cubic yards of raw materials to make 1 cubic yard of concrete.

The natural mixture of aggregates from a gravel pit, usually called "bank-run" gravel, is seldom suitable for concrete as the proportions of sand and gravel are not constant. It is better to buy the screened and recombined concrete mix. Tools and equipment needed are a small concrete mixer or mixing box if the concrete is to be mixed by hand, a deep metal wheelbarrow, a couple of No. 2 scoop shovels, and a convenient water connection. We purchased from our favorite mail-order house a mixer which handles a load of two cubic feet and ran it with the same little gas engine that pumped water from our well and ran the mud-mixer.

Now for the concrete mix itself. For ordinary conditions the mix used for foundations is one which attains an ultimate compression strength of 2,000 pounds per square inch in twenty-eight days. That, authoritative sources tell us, is to be had by using 6¼ gallons of water for each sack of cement (1 cubic foot) where *damp* aggregates are used, 5½ gallons to the sack of cement with *wet* aggregates, and 4¾ gallons if the aggregates are *very wet*. For some reason unknown to us the 6¼-gallon mix is generally referred to as a "7-gallon paste." Without going into the mysteries of concrete, we can say that the amount of water used with a given amount of cement determines the strength of the concrete. That is why it is necessary to observe whether the aggregates are damp, wet, or very wet before you start.

A suggested mix for a trial batch is 1 sack of cement, 2¾ cubic feet of sand, and 4 cubic feet of gravel or broken stone (not over 1½ inches in diameter). Use the amount of water specified for what you judge the moisture content of your aggregate to be. If this produces too soupy a mixture, add more sand and gravel. If it is too stiff, use less sand and gravel. Do not vary the amount of water.

We have recommended a small mixer, and obviously unless you have a very large one you are not going to be able to dump 6¼ gallons of water, a sack of cement, and approximately 7 cubic feet of aggregate into it all at once. The formula will have to be broken down to fit the load your mixer can take. In our case it worked out to 1 gallon, 5 pints water (measured in a marked pail), two No. 2 scoop shovels of cement, and 12½ shovels of the combined aggregate or concrete mix. This was for damp aggregate. When the aggregate was wet the amount of water used was 1 gallon, 3 pints, and where it was delivered dripping wet we cut the amount of mixing water to 5 quarts.

The water was poured in the turning mixer first, then the cement was added, and the aggregates were put in last. After all had mixed for a few minutes it was dumped into the wheelbarrow and taken to the form. The mixer load will make two wheelbarrow loads if the barrow is shallow.

A workable mix is one that can be poured into the forms without causing the ingredients to separate and will, with spading and tamping, flow into and fill all the angles and corners of the forms. There will be enough cement and sand in it to make a smooth surface without rough spots or holes when it has been properly tamped.

Concrete is poured in the forms in 6- to 12-inch layers and prodded and tamped so it will flow around the rods and pipes. A broomstick or other long handle with a flattened steel plate bolted on one end makes a good tool for working the cement in the forms. Corners and edges should get special attention from the tamper.

Ideally, the whole foundation of the house would be poured at once, thereby avoiding any construction seams, but with our limited time this was impossible so we divided our foundation into three sections: the bedroom, main room, and the balance of the house. If the work must stop before a section can be finished, the surface to be left unfinished should be leveled and roughened by scratching it up or some of the larger pieces of gravel may be set in it to project into the fresh layer. The rock "teeth" probably make the better bond but whichever is done it is important that the set concrete be washed to remove dirt or scum before the new is added.

The forms can be removed as soon as the concrete is hard enough to resist chipping and crumbling at the edges. In warm weather it will take only two or three days for the concrete to harden sufficiently to allow the stripping of the forms. Stakes are pulled, braces loosened, wire ties cut, and the long boards removed. If they are removed carefully they will be in good shape to use again.

Green concrete should be kept sprinkled and protected from hot suns and drying winds for a week or ten days after it is poured. If you must leave it during the week as we did, cover it with old sacks or burlap and wet them down well before you leave.

The pouring of the slab floors directly on the ground followed when the foundation was finished. In our house, the top of the finished floor is 4 inches below the top of the foundation and 2 inches above the outside grade level. Allowing 4 inches for the thickness of the concrete slab and 1½ inches for the thickness of the tile and mortar it was set in, our first step was to level the earth to 9½ inches below the top of the foundation.

We did not use waterproofed concrete for the floor slabs since our site is well drained and we planned to use a membrane of tar paper under the tile and mortar anyhow. Our floors stay dry, but were we doing it again we would omit the tar paper and treat the concrete with the same emulsion used to waterproof the bricks (1½ gallons of the emulsion to the sack of cement). This would be particularly advisable in any location that gets waterlogged.

In floor pouring, first fill or excavate as the need may be to the bottom level of the planned floor. In filling, place the dirt in 6-inch layers, wetting and tamping it well between each layer. Remove all organic matter such as roots and sticks. Measure the distance down from the top of the foundation and with a long straight board and mason's level check

Vertical steel rods at door and window openings are held in position by two-by-four uprights.

the ground for high and low spots. Time spent on getting an even level makes the rest of the job easier.

For convenience in pouring the concrete and in leveling and finishing the surface, the floor is divided into sections. These sections are divided with two-by-fours set on edge. Our 16′ x 24′ living room was divided into three 8′ x 16′ sections. Before leveling and staking the two-by-fours in place we cut and laid No. 4 gauge, electrically welded 6-inch-mesh reinforcing wire. We are not convinced that this was entirely necessary, but the cost in money or effort wasn't great and it is nice to know that the slab isn't likely to crack. The mesh was hard to cut until we hit on the happy expedient of borrowing a pair of small bolt cutters from a neighbor. As we laid the mest we overlapped the seams.

In putting in the floor forms we found it best to start by placing a two-by-four on edge along one side wall, staking it in place with small stakes and leveling it with little blocks and chips. The next two-by-four is staked on both sides to hold it in line about 8 feet or one-third of the distance across the room area. Putting a straight board or another two-by-four across first and second forms, block up the second until a level is obtained. Continue putting the two-by-fours across the room until the opposite side wall is reached. Check levels.

By dividing the floor into three sections and pouring outside sections first, a passage for the wheelbarrow is provided and it leaves room to maneuver the screed board as well. The screed board is a straight-edged board long enough to reach across one section of the floor; a piece of 1″ x 6″ is suitable. When a few loads of concrete have been dumped in the farthest corner of a section, stand this board on edge, resting it on the 2″ x 4″ forms and draw it back and forth in a sawing motion, moving it ahead at the same time. Strike the concrete off to the level of the forms. Fill any low spots with the shovel and continue until the section is filled. Fill outside sections first, center section last. Where wire mesh is used it should be raised by pulling it up to the center of the concrete as it is poured. Before the concrete sets, pull stakes and the forms along the foundation wall. Lift the mesh gently, if mesh is used, and with a trowel fill the crack left by the removal of the two-by-four and smooth it off with a small wooden float or a mason's trowel. Wooden floats are smooth rectangles of 1-foot board with handles on the back; they are used to smooth the concrete to a rough finish—all that is needed when the floor is to have a finished surface of tile. When the concrete of the outer section is hard enough to hold your weight on a board laid across it, walk out on it, raise the center forms, and fill the resulting gaps.

The mixture for the floor is a little richer than that used for the foundation. It is a 3,000 pound mix, obtained by using 5½ gallons of water to a sack of cement and damp aggregates; a 1 to 2¼ to 3 mix. For a load in our small mixer the trial batch, using damp aggregates, was 1 gallon, 3 pints of water, 2 shovels of cement, and 10½ shovels of the concrete mix (4½ parts sand, 6 parts broken rock). With wet aggregates the trial batch would have used 5 quarts of water. Had they been very wet only 9 pints of water would have been needed. The mixture should be rather stiff for floors, stiff enough to require some spading and tamping to get it to settle. With a good mixture there will not be any surplus water standing on the floor. When it is hard enough to get out on by laying a board on it, compact and smooth the surface with a wooden float.

For proper curing a freshly poured floor should be kept moist for at least a week. One way to do this is to dam up the door openings with a few shovels of earth and then flood the floor. Any flooding must wait, however, until the concrete is hard enough to stand the action of the water or else the cement will wash out and leave the surface pitted.

To cover 100 square feet of floor to a depth of 4 inches will take 8 sacks of cement and 1½ cubic yards of concrete mix using the 1 to 2¼ to 3 mix.

We set bolts to hold the plates for the stud partitions as the floor was poured. To keep them from being a menace we hung a shiny tin can over each one.

Floors are seldom completely finished before the roof is on as they might get marred during the rest of the construction; for now the floor can be considered done. Mixing a few batches of concrete should be nothing awesome and in truth there is nothing mysterious about it. Although it is well to keep a watch on proportions, the main thing is to get some cement in every batch as we were once told by an old contractor. More specific information is contained in the following booklets: *Foundations for Farm Buildings,* Farmers' Bulletin No. 1869; *Foundation Walls and Basements of Concrete,* Form 12, Portland Cement Association, 33 West Grand Ave., Chicago, Illinois.

V

Laying the Walls of the Adobe House

WHEN the bricks are all made and stacked, when the plans and working drawings are clear and complete, and when the foundation is well set, the real fun of building with adobe begins. You'll still be using your brains and muscles but the laying of the walls is undoubtedly the most impressive and satisfying part of the entire building.

Very few tools are needed for this part of the job and you will have most of them already. You will need a mason's large triangular trowel, a small triangular trowel for pointing, a 4-foot wooden level, a sturdy piece of line (seine twine is excellent), and an old hatchet for chopping bricks to odd sizes. If you are using the vertical steel rods by door and window openings and are building a wall one brick thick, you will need something to bore holes through the bricks that pass over the rods. We used a carpenter's brace with an old 1-inch bit. With a little elbow grease the bit went through easily enough unless it hit a stone. In that

47

case either the rock was pecked out with an old star drill or the brick was abandoned. The whole business of measuring, drilling the hole, and then lifting the brick and threading it down over the rod is not as hard as it sounds and it is fine earthquake insurance. An easier way would be to cast a few 4″ x 6″ x 18″ bricks which would be half as wide as the full brick and use two of them in the wall around rods.

Before the actual bricklaying is started, door jambs are put in place and braced to a true vertical beside the door openings. We used 2″ x 12″ kiln-dried redwood planks for our door jambs, and since they were full wall width they face the door openings completely. These jambs were spiked to two-by-fours which were in turn spiked to the nailing-blocks provided for them in the foundation.

The mortar we used for laying bricks was made of cement, concrete sand (plaster sand is too fine), emulsified asphalt, and water. Proportions were 1 part cement, 2½ parts sand, plus stabilizer and enough water to make it of mortar consistency; 1½ gallons of the stabilizing emulsion is used to each sack (1 cubic foot) of cement.

To figure quantities for your mixing arrangement or "batch," remember that seven full shovels, if the shovel is the common No. 2 scoop, will average 1 cubic foot and that it takes 1½ gallons of emulsion to the cubic foot of cement. The sand and cement are first stirred together dry. When these are thoroughly mixed, the water with the proper amount of stabilizer is added and all stirred until a smooth, buttery mix results. Since the amount of water used depends on the moisture already in the sand, it can only be determined by making a trial batch or two. As the concrete mortar sets up fast, it is best to mix only a small amount at a time unless you have a large crew of bricklayers. These small batches are best mixed with a garden hoe in a metal wheelbarrow. Larger batches may be mixed in a regular plaster mixing box or a plaster mixer. A concrete mixer isn't very satisfactory for mortar.

The original adobe house builders used mud mortar made of nothing but earth and water. Some adobes are now being laid with a mortar of earth, water, and the waterproofing stabilizer. This has the advantage of being cheaper and somewhat easier to work since it doesn't set up as fast as concrete mortar, but it is conceded that the best bond and the strongest building is achieved with waterproofed concrete mortar.

With a batch of mortar ready, the bricklaying may commence.

Sprinkle a short section of the top of the foundation and a few bricks with water. With shovel or trowel, spoon some mortar near a front corner of the foundation, using the trowel to smooth it to an approximate half-inch thickness. Keep the mortar in from the wall edges as otherwise it will just slop over the sides when the brick is set in it. Cracks and gaps in the mortar are filled in later. Place a brick on a corner and slide it around in the mortar until it is square with the foundation. Check it vertically as well by holding the long level against the foundation wall. If the brick is warped and rocks when pressure is put on it, lift the low side or edge and push extra mortar under it with the trowel until it sets firm and level. When a few bricks are in place on the first corner, move to the opposite corner and lay a few there. Stretch a line between the two corners (small nails driven in the bricks will hold it) and check the level. As each layer of bricks, or "course" as it is called by masons, is laid with the top of the course even with the guide line, the line is moved up for the next course. Except for corners, which may be built up to support guide lines, brick courses should run level around the entire building, including brick partition walls.

To get corners solid, start at the end of each row with a whole brick. Begin the first course with the corner brick laid full length on the front wall; the corner brick on the second course will run full length on the side wall and so on up the corner. If less than full-size bricks must be used to make the course come out even, make the needed adjustment along in the middle somewhere. Adobes are easily cut with a hatchet, even a dull one. Allow space for approximately a half-inch of mortar between the bricks in the row and also between the courses. As the wall rises, check it frequently to keep it vertical and to keep the top of each row as level as possible. The bricks will vary considerably, so that no part of it will be as true and even as a wall of common brick laid by experienced masons; nor should it be, for the charm of the adobe wall lies in its irregularities.

When the first layer of brick covers the top of the foundation, two strands of ordinary barbed wire are laid parallel along on top of the bricks and fastened to stay 2 inches in from each wall face with common wire staples. The wires are carried around the entire course. Where breaks in the wire occur, an 18-inch overlap should be allowed. It should never be spliced or overlapped at corners. When wires reach

Notched bricks fit around redwood two-by-four and reinforcing rod at door openings; note strands of barbed wire (LEFT). Window frames of 2″ x 12″ redwood are placed directly on the pre-cast concrete sill; notched bricks fit around the two-by-fours as at door openings (RIGHT).

the door jambs or window frames, run them up along the back of the jamb for 18 inches and staple them securely. These strands of barbed wire are placed between every sixth course of bricks, above and below wall openings, and in the last mortar joint below the bond beam.

On the last mortar joint below the bond beam make extra wire loops around the two strands, placing them about 3 feet apart, and allow them to extend up through spaces between bricks in the last course. These loops should be long enough to be fastened around the reinforcing rod in the bond beam.

As the bricks go in the wall, give the bottom of each a sprinkle of water and also sprinkle the top of the previously laid row before the new mortar is shoveled on. This strengthens the bond between brick and mortar and is easiest done with an old garden watering pot. Watch the joints in the row, staggering them so joint does not come directly over joint.

When the lower window levels are reached (keep an eye on your elevation plans), set the window sills in the wall. Sills and lintels may be of timber or concrete. In either material they should be of full-wall thickness and extend along it for at least 9 inches on both sides of the opening. Some builders recommend a 12-inch overhang. We used reinforced concrete in a 1 to $2\frac{1}{4}$ to 3 mix for both sills and lintels; they were poured directly into the wall. To do this we set bricks 9 inches away from outside jamb dimensions and clamped a 1″ x 6″ board between them on both sides. Furniture clamps held them in place. As the form was only one brick (4 inches) deep, tops of the 6-inch boards were placed on a level with the tops of the bricks that made the ends of the form. The bottom of the form was simply the previous course of bricks. As the concrete was poured three half-inch steel rods the full length of the form were laid in it.

The window frames, 2″ x 12″ redwood planks, were set on top of the hardened concrete sills and braced temporarily. The plank facings were spiked to redwood two-by-fours as was done on the door frames. Notched bricks made for this purpose were fitted around the two-by-fours and the steel rods running vertically along window openings. Crevices were carefully filled with mortar. (See photograph, page 50.)

As the walls go up, attention must also be paid to the location of light switches and any outlet boxes above baseboard level. Conduit pipe will

Two strands of barbed wire are stapled on the top of the first course of bricks and between every sixth course thereafter.

have to be worked into the wall for these switches and outlets and from them up to a junction box above the bond beam. After struggling to fit bricks around boxes and bends in the conduit we finally clamped more board forms across between bricks as we did in the window sills and filled the vacant spaces with concrete. When the walls were painted the difference was unnoticeable.

When we reached the top of our door and window openings we had in most instances also reached the top of our brick wall. Where the windows did not reach to the bottom of the bond beam more forms were made as with the sills, the only difference being that the top of the window frame, a redwood plank again, acted as the bottom of the form, which was filled with concrete reinforced with steel rods.

Interior brick partition walls rise at the same rate as the exterior walls. They interlock with one another by means of key bricks set where the walls meet. Fireplaces, whether of adobe or other material, should also go up as the walls do. How we built our fireplaces is described in the last portion of this chapter.

When the last brick has been set in the wall it is time to think of the collar beam, the binding for the top of the wall. The forms are easily made; 1″ x 10″ boards nailed to the adobe so that the top edges are level and at least 6 inches above the last layer of bricks all around do the trick. If the top of the wall didn't come out exactly even, and chances are that it didn't, this is the time to level it up before the roof plate goes on. Wire ties hold the form together, and 12-inch spreaders hold it apart as in the foundation forms. Two half-inch reinforcing rods run through the beam, going continuously around corners and lapping at breaks for at least 18 inches. These horizontal rods are fastened to the vertical rods which bend over to go into the bond beam and the loops of barbed wire extending through from the last mortar joint are twisted around them as well. Over wall openings the collar beam should be reinforced with three half-inch rods.

Bolts 6½″ x ⅝″ are set 4 feet apart in the concrete of the collar beam to hold the 2″ x 8″ roof plate down. Seats for the tie beams should be left in the collar beam too. There are two of these tie beams (8″ x 8″ redwood) crossing our main room. A base of concrete was poured in the last course of bricks for the heavy beams and more large steel bolts were imbedded in the block to fasten them down.

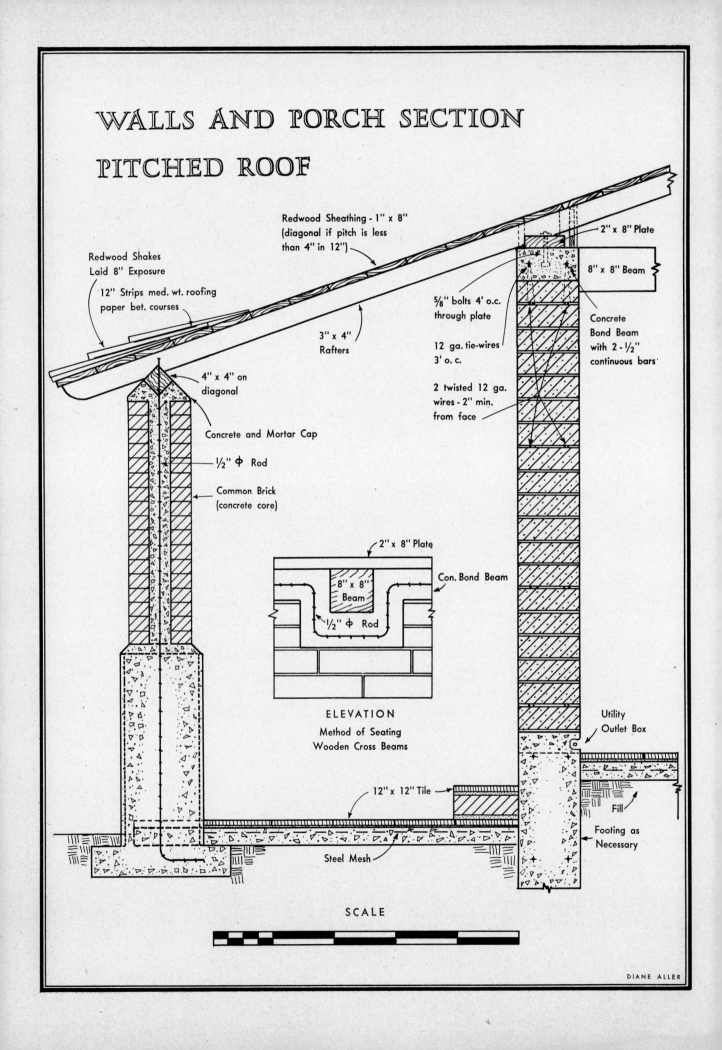

WALLS AND PORCH SECTION
PITCHED ROOF

Redwood Sheathing - 1" x 8"
(diagonal if pitch is less
than 4" in 12")

2" x 8" Plate

Redwood Shakes
Laid 8" Exposure

8" x 8" Beam

12" Strips med. wt. roofing
paper bet. courses

5/8" bolts 4' o.c.
through plate

Concrete
Bond Beam
with 2 - 1/2"
continuous bars

3" x 4"
Rafters

12 ga. tie-wires
3' o. c.

4" x 4" on
diagonal

2 twisted 12 ga.
wires - 2" min.
from face

Concrete and Mortar Cap

1/2" Φ Rod

Common Brick
(concrete core)

2" x 8" Plate

Con. Bond Beam

8" x 8"
Beam

1/2" Φ Rod

ELEVATION

Method of Seating
Wooden Cross Beams

Utility
Outlet Box

12" x 12" Tile

Fill

Steel Mesh

Footing as
Necessary

SCALE

DIANE ALLER

The concrete mix used for the bond beam was the same as that for the floors and sills, a 1 to $2\frac{1}{4}$ to 3 mixture. Getting batches of the wet stuff nine feet or so off the ground and in the overhead forms was a bit of a problem. After pondering the possibilities of using various hoists, we abandoned that approach and built a movable platform and ramp. We ran the wheelbarrow up the ramp and from that point shoveled the concrete into the form. Although it was strenuous, no one of us is any the worse for it now.

The collar beam takes in chimneys too. In our house we have two which run from foundation to above the roof peak. One large chimney holds two flues, one for the inside and one for the outside fireplace. These fireplaces are built back to back, and both hearths are above floor level. That of the inside fireplace is $2\frac{1}{2}$ feet off the floor and the opening is just a little over 2 feet square. In dream houses the fireplace is usually very large and to many a 2-foot one will seem dinky, as indeed it would appear if it were conventionally placed at floor level. As it is, higher on the wall, it gives the effect of being larger; it provides the glowing fire that is still the best center of interest for a living room and is at the same time small enough not to dominate it. We sometimes cook on this hearth and find it convenient as well as quaint. The firebox is slightly deeper than that of the average small fireplace and it will take a surprisingly large chunk of wood.

The outside fireplace is a combination barbecue grill and fireplace and for easy cooking this hearth is also above the floor.

As most of the "works" of both fireplaces were outside the wall, building of the wall was carried on until the height of the fireplace arch was reached. Heavy 2″ x 8″ planks were set in the wall openings as temporary guides to laying the sidewall bricks.

Common bricks were used for the outside walls of the barbecue grill and chimney and for facing the inside fireplace. The outside walls of the barbecue were made two bricks thick and spaces between these common brick walls and our adobe house wall were filled with rubble (broken adobe bricks, other bricks, and stones) and mortar. Vertical reinforcing rods were embedded in the foundation for the two fireplaces; they pass up through the structure on either side of the flue lining.

When the floors of the fireplaces were reached, firebrick was used for floors and sidewalls of the fireboxes. To assure the proper slope on the curved backs we built curved forms of laths and laid the firebrick to it, removing the form after the mortar had set. Lintels to support the bricks over the openings were pieces of $\frac{1}{2}''$ x $3\frac{1}{2}''$ angle iron. No dampers were used in our fireplaces as we have seen too many of them warped from heat and no longer useful after a few years. They are usually removed and not replaced when that happens—but make your own decision about dampers. Many experts declare them essential. We think our fireplaces work very well without them.

Adobe bricks may face the fireplace and form chimney breasts, but they should not be used near extreme heat nor should they be used where edges would get hard wear because they will chip. For this reason we used common pink bricks to face our fireplaces. We used brick ties, little metal gadgets, to hold the single layer of small bricks to the adobe wall. A rough piece of lumber was put up for a "stand-in" until the carved oak mantel strip was finished.

Dimensions of openings, throat, and flue were taken from Farmers' Bulletin No. 1889, *Fireplaces and Chimneys.* This is a very concise and helpful booklet. A later edition, Farmers' Bulletin No. 1649, *Construction of Chimneys and Fireplaces,* is also of value to the amateur fireplace builder. They are both available through the Department of Agriculture at Washington, D.C.

Two $8\frac{1}{2}''$ x $17''$ fire-clay flue liners were placed in the chimney and the common-brick work carried up with the adobe walls to the last course under the bond beam. The bond beam included the chimney, as has been said before, and was tied in with short lengths of half-inch rod.

Mortar made of 1 part cement, $\frac{1}{2}$ part lime, and $4\frac{1}{2}$ parts sand was used to lay the common bricks. Common bricks are always soaked in water for a time before they are laid to insure a good bond between brick and mortar. Laying these small bricks came to be considered "woman's work" on our house and as a consequence I did nearly all of this with Diane as my hod carrier. As I always put more zeal than accuracy into my work it went fast, and consequently my chimneys stand picturesquely if not truly vertical.

A brick hammer is a good thing to have for laying these small bricks. They should have a couple of smart raps to set them in the mortar so some sort of hammer is essential. Regular brick hammers have a brick cutting edge handy for cutting bricks to odd sizes although that can be done with any hammer and an old cold chisel. The lime in the mortar is a little rough on hands so a pair of stout gloves is another useful accessory for the lady bricklayer.

The chimney for our kitchen-stove flue presented quite a problem. An adobe partition wall ended abruptly to open a small hall (see floor plan), and we wanted to brace this wall, really only a spur, at the same time making a projection that would form a small alcove for the range. A hot-water storage tank needed a place to hide as well. As a solution to all of these problems we cast a concrete-walled closet, the walls of which are 4 inches thick, reinforced; and the top is 1 foot thick and is tied to the collar beam with short steel rods. Holes for the pipes to and from the water-storage tank were made when the closet was poured, and a 6-inch fire-clay patent flue and a length of fire-clay pipe were cast in position for the stove pipe and ventilation flue from the kitchen stove. After the walls were up, a common brick chimney was built on top of the collar beam over this structure. As roof level was attained on both chimneys, work was stopped on them to await construction of the roof so that flashing could be installed where chimneys and roof came together.

It was then, after our day's work was done, that we would sit within the walls of our unfinished house before a fire in our unfinished fireplace and look up at the stars. Even with only the sky as a roof we sat there in the firelight and could get the "feel" of our house. We knew that it was good.

VI

Roofing the Adobe House

AFTER the forms were stripped from the concrete collar beam, the large tie beams were placed in the top of the wall and bolted down. The beams had been carved before they were placed. With them up, construction of the roof was begun.

Before so much as a rafter was cut, however, the style, pitch, and framing details in general were worked out on the drawing board. As a result our house has what is known as a gable-and-valley roof with a one-sixth pitch.

A simple gable roof has two slopes meeting at a center ridge forming a gable. Our gable-and-valley roof is a combination of two gable roofs meeting at right angles. The valley is the meeting place of the two slopes running at right angles to one another. The pitch of the roof is the degree of slope from the ridge to the roof plate and this may be expressed in

59

two ways: the ratio to total building width of the total rise to the ridge; the number of inches of vertical rise to each foot of horizontal run.

In the first instance, the ratio may be one-half, one-fourth or one-sixth because the measured height from the level of the roof plate to the top of the ridge board is one-half, one-fourth, or one-sixth of the total width of the building. Our house has a one-sixth pitch as the main span (width) is 18 feet, the rise (distance between ridge and roof plate) is 3 feet. Eighteen divides by three to six parts, hence a one-sixth pitch.

Referring to the second way of describing roof pitch, our roof is also known as a "4 in 12." These figures state the number of inches of vertical rise to each foot of horizontal run. The "run" is one-half the house span. "Rise per foot of run" figures are used again and again in roof building; therefore, on planning your roof, have the rise per foot in even inches to simplify greatly the laying out and rafter cutting.

We chose this slope of roof because we wanted it as low as was practical and a roof of 18½ degrees, our 4 in 12, was the flattest recommended for shakes or shingles. Moreover, anything flatter on an adobe house is said to require diagonal sheathing, which we didn't want because it would be visible inside most rooms in the house. In heavy snow country there are roof construction problems other than appearance, and local practice should be followed. The square and cross-cut and rip saws are the important tools in framing a roof, and of course your familiar hammer. The square is used to lay off the angles of the rafters and is the important tool. Years ago, when building a playhouse for Diane, we purchased a nice new shiny square which had a booklet titled *Stanley Rafter and Framing Squares* wrapped around one end of it. We knew that carpenters figured lengths of rafters, angles of rafter cuts, and possibly even their income taxes with this wondrous tool, so with the square and the booklet in our hands we prepared to get to the bottom of some of these secrets. It was disillusioning to find that our square did not have the roofing and framing tables but tables for figuring braces and board feet. It was only a common, or garden variety square, not the de luxe model that the attached booklet had led us to believe it was. As a consequence, Diane's playhouse was framed by the use of square root and the good old hypotenuse of the right-angled triangle.

The roof on our adobe house was planned on paper the same way, but when the walls were up they were far from mathematically perfect.

As a matter of fact, they were so far out in places along the wall plate as to throw a hypotenuse or even a framing square into a tailspin. So we just did what we imagined a Mexican builder would do and used a long straight board to take actual measurements from the ridge board to the roof plate, remembering that measurements for common rafters are taken along a line down the center of the rafter, each rafter being measured separately. This worked, but we still believe that a framing square would save time, particularly in figuring the cuts on the valley rafters and the angles on the valley "jacks." We picked the angles off with a bevel gauge. With or without a framing square, that little booklet put out by the Stanley Rule and Level Plant of New Britain, Connecticut, on rafters and roof framing is a valuable reference that is free and still available.

Getting back to the actual roof construction, the 2″ x 8″ roof plate was set in one inch from the outside face on top of the collar beam and fastened there with nuts and washers to the bolts that had been set in the concrete previously. Planks were held in position on top of the bolts and rapped with a hammer to mark the bolt's shank so the holes could be bored accurately. At corners and at splices, half-lap joints were made and nailed together. Next, 2″ x 6″ uprights were set on the cross beams at the center of the span. Braced temporarily, a 2″ x 6″ ridge board was bolted to them. Joints in the ridge board were spliced with half-lap joints and bolted together. This ridge board was later covered to resemble a beam where it would show inside the house. The false beam also concealed wiring and outlet boxes for the overhead fixtures but a heavier piece could have been used and left as it was.

As common rafters are measured along a center line at the side of the rafter, the height of the ridge board must be the rise plus half the thickness of the rafter measured along the diagonal of the top cut. As we used 3″ x 4″ rafters, this was an additional $2\frac{1}{8}$ inches. In turn, one-half the thickness of the ridge board must be subtracted when figuring the length of the rafter from the ridge to the heel or seat cut. At the intersection of the valley and the main roof, the ridge board must be left long enough to hold the valley rafters. As valley rafters run at an angle of 45 degrees to the common rafters, this additional length should be the run plus one-half the rafter thickness. The run of valley rafters is not the same as that of the common rafters; it is the hypotenuse of the

*Brick and concrete porch columns have been built to height and the rafters
are in place ready for roof sheathing.*

square whose sides are equal to the run of the common rafter. Valley rafters are measured along a center line at the top. It is safer to have the ridge board a little long as it can be sawn to exact length when all the rafters are up.

After the wall plate and ridge boards were up we built the masonry porch columns to height and set a ridge plate, a 4″ x 4″ laid diamond-wise on top of them. The height of the porch columns was determined from the drawings, and we checked on the job by figuring the distance from the wall plate to the center of the porch plate, using the 4- in 12-inch ratio since the pitch of our roof was uniform from ridge to the edge of the porch. The porch roof didn't flatten out.

The overhang allowed on our rafters is 1 foot measured on a horizontal line from the side of the building. There are at least two ways of finding out how much to allow past the seat cut for this overhang— the hard way is to get the hypotenuse of the angle, base 12 inches, altitude 4 inches or 12.64 inches; the easier way is to measure across the square between the 12-inch mark on one leg and the 4-inch mark on the other with a rule. The answer will be 12⅝ inches or very close to it. The answer on your roof will depend on how wide the eaves are and the rise per foot.

We curved the ends of our rafters by cutting them to a close angle with a saw and then rounding them over; it went quickly and easily, with a sharp 1½-inch wood chisel and mallet.

The rafters were nailed to the ridge board and to the wall plate with 20-penny common nails. Care was taken to space them 2 feet apart on centers at both wall plate and ridge.

The next step was to cut the uprights at the ends on the gables. They were cut to the by-now familiar angle to fit under the rafters and were spaced along the wall plate 2 feet on centers; the bottoms were toenailed to the wall plate and the tops were nailed to the outside roof rafter. Rough sheathing, salvaged from the lumber used in concrete forms, was nailed horizontally over these uprights. If there is to be an attic, holes are cut in the rough sheathing for the installation of ventilators. We put the finish siding on next. This could have come later, but for amateur builders it is easier to mark, cut, and nail this siding before the roof sheathing is on. We used 1″ x 8″ redwood applied vertically, the bottom end of each board rounded to make a scallop which came just below the

Construction of chimneys is held up awaiting completion of roof framing and sheathing (TOP). *Shakes are laid 8 inches to the weather over 12-inch strips of roofing paper; note guide strip* (BOTTOM).

wall plate. If the lumber has been surfaced on both sides, or is to be rough on both sides, waste and extra work will be avoided as the angle can be cut, the board turned over, and the same angle used for the matching board on the other half of the gable.

The solid roof sheathing may go on when the gables are finished. We nailed 1″ x 8″ redwood sheathing, with one side and two edges surfaced, to the rafters with 8-penny common galvanized nails. We sorted our sheathing boards and used those with the fewest defects for those rooms that were to be open to the roof. A little extra was allowed to overhang at the gable ends to be trimmed off evenly later.

The total length of the roof, including the overhang, should be in multiples of two since that is the way boards come from the lumber yard. In building our adobe garage we learned that adobe bricks can be chopped and cast in odd sizes to piece out a wall to any length, but boards can't be stretched, so think of lumber in even-numbered lengths and let wall lengths take care of themselves.

Openings for plumbing vent pipes are made in the roof sheathing as it is laid. Chimneys can be built up now, the built-in flashing bent back out of the way to await the laying of the shakes or other roof covering. A little space is left where the sheathing would meet the chimneys to allow room for expansion due to temperature changes; this space also serves as fire protection and to keep the sheathing free of the chimney if it does any settling.

Another addition to your collection of building booklets should be Farmers' Bulletin No. 1751, *Roof Coverings for Farm Buildings and Their Repair*. This goes into details on flashing more thoroughly than Farmers' Bulletin No. 1889, *Fireplaces and Chimneys*. While on the subject of flashing, it should be said that the valleys of the roof should be covered with a strip of corrosion-resisting metal at least 14 inches wide —7 inches on either side of the valley. Copper is de luxe but galvanized sheet metal will do.

After the sheathing is on and the ends trimmed, the pairs of rafters on the outside gable ends of the roof are nailed up. These "beauty rafters" (so called because they do not support anything but do provide a finish for what otherwise would be a raw edge of loose board ends) are simple to cut because there are only the top and bottom angles to make. They are a problem to hold in place under the roof edge while they are being nailed. We pulled them up with ropes and held them in place with our versatile furniture clamps until they were secured with nails.

Now we were ready for the final roof covering. We used redwood shakes, but shingles or tile or any roof covering could be used. We considered tile, and tile does make a lovely roof for adobe houses, but a stray sentence read in some of our research to the effect that roofs on the early California adobes were of tile in good clay regions and of redwood shakes in the redwood country caused us to conform to tradition and choose shakes. The color, weather-darkened, and the rugged shadow lines make us glad of our choice.

A shake is simply a split shingle in a larger size. Here in Cauifornia they are split from clear redwood, in the Pacific Northwest from cedar. Other parts of the country probably use local woods which split readily. Because of their durable qualities, both cedar and redwood make good shakes. Cedar weathers to a silvery grey, redwood to a deep brown and is somewhat more fire-resistant than untreated cedar.

Our shakes were 23 inches to 24 inches long and in random widths from 4 inches to 8 inches. Instead of being split on both sides as they were in pioneer days they are split on the top side and taper-sawn on the under side so they don't curl. The butt ends vary in thickness from $\frac{1}{2}$ to $1\frac{1}{2}$ inches, tapering to about $\frac{1}{8}$ inch at the top end.

Our "4 in 12" was the minimum slope for shakes, so we took extreme care in laying them to make a good, tight roof. Waterproof roofing paper was laid in strips under each course of shakes, the paper overlapping in the same manner as the rows of shakes and concealed by them. Nails used were 5-penny hot-dipped, zinc-coated to resist rust. The length of the nail is important where the roof sheathing is seen from inside. We were pounding away happily on the roof of the garage-guesthouse when someone inside observed that the nail points were coming through! Every one of them had to be clipped off with nail clippers, not an easy or interesting task.

More details as we go. Let us start laying the shakes. Begin in a lower left-hand corner and lay a double course of shakes, breaking all joints at least $1\frac{1}{2}$ inches (more is better) and allowing an overhang of at least 1 inch at eaves and rakes (sides). Shakes are spaced approximately a half-inch apart to allow for expansion, for they will buckle when they get soaking wet if they are laid to fit closely. On the second layer of the first course, be sure to keep all nail heads back at least 8½ inches because none should be left exposed. The head of the nail should be just flush with the surface of the shake; resist that temptation to give it just one more whack or you'll bruise wood fibers and possibly cause your roof to leak.

After the double course is on the edge of the roof, measure back 8 inches and lightly tack some long, thin slats across the roof in a straight line as a gauge for the next course. A chalk line is usually snapped across the roof to make a mark to lay shingles to, but it doesn't give a clear line on shakes—too rough. Moreover, shakes are likely to be any and all angles across the butt—part of their charm—and the slat makes the best guide line.

The next step is tacking a 12-inch strip of medium-weight roofing paper along the upper side of the guide line. A 36-inch roll of roofing paper can be cut in three parts with an old saw, using a little kerosene to lubricate the cut, or it may be unrolled on a flat surface, marked with a chalk line, and cut with scissors or knife. Keep the paper strip back of the guide line so none of it will show, tack it in a few places, and begin laying the next course of shakes over the paper. Rain may back up under shakes in a driving storm, but with the paper layer between courses it runs out again. It is a little extra bother, although very little extra expense, and it seemed to us worth the trouble.

In the valleys, shakes should be sawn to conform to a straight line down the angle of the valley. All nails should be kept back at least a full inch from the exposed edge. A guide line insures neatness. The metal-lined valley should be wide enough to carry the expected volume of water off rapidly, and should widen slightly toward the gutter. Our gutters are approximately 5 inches wide and should have been wider because they get clogged up with leaves if we don't check them occasionally. A clogged run-off will cause water to back up and penetrate an otherwise satisfactory roof.

As the ridge is reached a course is brought up on one side and sawed off evenly; the other side is brought up to lap over it and then sawed in a line with the ridge. As a line of shakes 5 to 6 inches wide will be used to make a cap, the last regular course of shakes should be at least 13 or 14 inches long. To arrive at this, the last few rows may vary in the amount left to the weather. Number of "inches to the weather" refers to the part of the shingle or shake left exposed. The ridge is capped with a row of narrow shakes laid 8 inches to the weather running along the ridge at right angles to the rest of the shakes. Work from both ends toward the center until the shakes overlap at the middle. The meeting place is covered with a shake cap just long enough to cover the tips, 5 or 6 inches.

Metal gutters were not to be had when we were ready to put up our gutters so we used wooden V-troughs made of old flooring. Instead of downspouts we merely let the ends of our wooden gutters project from the house for about 18 inches. We had planned to replace the gutters and provide downspouts, but we have changed our minds now as the ones we have do the work and seem to suit the house better than metal ones would. We noticed that many of the houses in Mexico had no gutters at roof edges at all; instead, cobbled troughs ran around the base of the house and directed the water away from it.

When the roof was finished to the last nail, we turned back to our bricklaying and built the chimneys up to within 4 inches of the tops of the projecting flue lining, capping the top row of bricks with two inches of cement mortar. The mortar was sloped downward from the flue lining to the outer edge of the chimney. With this, our roof, the last big job of our house building, was finished.

VII

Plumbing in the Adobe House

As WE KNEW next to nothing about plumbing when we began our house, we accepted the published invitation in the Sears, Roebuck catalogue to discuss our plumbing problems with them by mail. According to the description of this service, all one needed to do was send a sketch of the proposed floor plan and the number of fixtures desired and a mastermind in the store's employ would determine the number of nipples, street ells, and other fantastically designated pipe oddments one would need and send them on. They would also send instructions for installing these and a certificate, in color, proclaiming that your plumbing came from Sears. That was enough for us and the discussions by mail began. Our correspondence with the plumbing department grew to such voluminous proportions and so complicated that we eventually tired of it. I think they were tired of it too. For one thing, it got so a new

PLUMBING & SEWAGE DISPOSAL SYSTEM

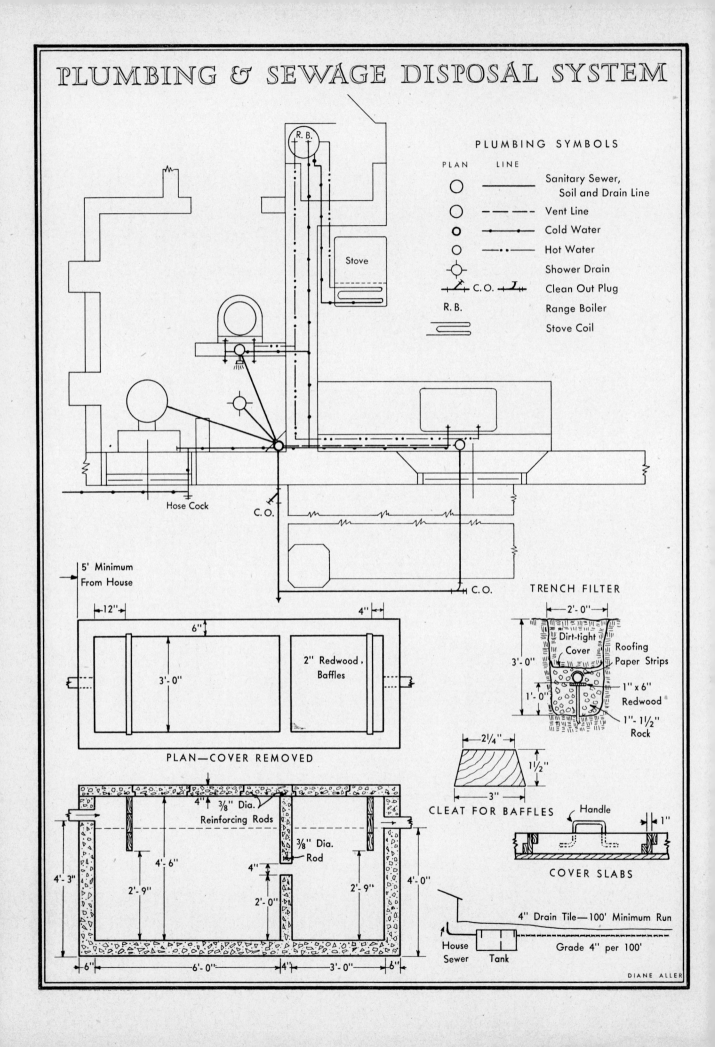

PLUMBING SYMBOLS

PLAN LINE

Sanitary Sewer, Soil and Drain Line

Vent Line

Cold Water

Hot Water

Shower Drain

C.O. Clean Out Plug

R.B. Range Boiler

Stove Coil

Stove

R.B.

Hose Cock

C.O.

C.O.

5' Minimum From House

12"   4"

6"

3'-0"

2" Redwood, Baffles

PLAN—COVER REMOVED

4"   3/8" Dia. Reinforcing Rods

3/8" Dia. Rod

4'-6"

4"

2'-9"   2'-9"

2'-0"

4'-3"   4'-0"

6"   6'-0"   4"   3'-0"   6"

TRENCH FILTER

2'-0"

Dirt-tight Cover

Roofing Paper Strips

3'-0"

1'-0"

1" x 6" Redwood

1"-1 1/2" Rock

2 1/4"

1 1/2"

3"

CLEAT FOR BAFFLES

Handle   1"

COVER SLABS

4" Drain Tile—100' Minimum Run

House Sewer   Tank   Grade 4" per 100'

DIANE ALLER

plumbing consultant would answer every time we wrote. We think that the old one resigned rather than face our problem: putting in plumbing without recourse to hollow walls and space under floors. Every one of those plumbing consultants insisted we put vents in the walls and sewer outlets under the house, and we patiently started over with every one of them and tried to explain why we couldn't do those things in an adobe house. Each time we heard from Sears a new man would beg us to submit a new sketch to him. The last one gave up and recommended that "a licensed plumber be employed. . . . . we feel that this is quite a job to tackle." The sissy!

We decided to tackle it anyway and had the nipples and street ells and a magnificent assortment of other odd shapes in soil pipe and galvanized pipe sent on. In due time they all arrived. The fixtures were crated but every bit of the other plumbing, except the long lengths of soil pipe which were thoughtfully sent first to our city apartment, came in huge gunny sacks. Now buying plumbing from Sears, Roebuck & Company may be full of pitfalls when neither you nor that redoubtable mail-order house knows exactly what is to be done, but we kept right on doing it.

One advantage was that we had described our problem so often and in such detail that it finally became fairly clear to us, if not to anyone else; furthermore one of the consultants had forwarded a very convenient small booklet for the amateur plumber. It ignored masonry or adobe houses but told how to put plumbing in all sorts of places. The average book on plumbing is not very good unless you are considering plumbing as a life work.

We dipped into the huge gunny sacks and began. True, we had some of our plumbing pieces left over when we were finished and still have no idea where they were intended to go, but clean water comes into the house, waste water leaves it, and the vent pipes carry off fumes. We are not dissatisfied with our grab-bag plumbing.

You will need some specialized tools to put in your own plumbing, but they are not so specialized that they won't prove handy to have around a country place for years to come. You will need a pipe vise, a pipe-threading set capable of threading pipe up to and including 1-inch pipe, a good hack saw, a lead melting-pot and dipper, several caulking chisels, and a yarning iron for tamping oakum in soil-pipe joints, an asbestos joint runner, and a couple of pipe wrenches. If you haven't an idea what some of these even look like, look them up in that dictionary of merchandise—the general catalogue of a large mail-order house.

Before the plumbing can be planned, a slight knowledge of what a plumbing system is will be needed by the planner. To put it simply, a plumbing system is an arrangement of pipes that bring clean water into the house through the faucets of the various fixtures and carry overflow out through drains; there are more pipes that carry the dirty waste water away from the house to the sewer or sewage-disposal system. Admittedly an adobe house without plumbing would be far easier to build, if not to live in, but putting in plumbing isn't as difficult and mysterious as most of us have been led to believe.

The installation of a plumbing system consists of three steps: installing soil pipe to carry drainage, installing galvanized water-supply pipes to carry hot and cold water to fixtures, and finally installing the fixtures themselves (sinks, tubs, toilets, etc.) and connecting them to supply and waste pipes.

In adobe houses with concrete floors poured directly on the ground as ours were, certain parts of the plumbing are done before the floors are poured, others when the walls are going up, and still others much later. These things should be considered first in the planning (see chapter iii, "Planning the Adobe House"), and then a plumbing plan and program should be worked out to insure that steps in the installation of the plumbing are taken at the proper times in the house construction.

Let us consider the drainage part of the system first. In our house it consists of a cast-iron soil pipe, one end of it going out through the foundation to the septic tank, the other end continuing right up through the roof. The part extending through the roof is called the "vent" and is a smaller pipe than the drainage end since it carries nothing but gas fumes. Before it goes through the roof and becomes a vent, this vertical iron pipe is called a "stack." Connected to and entering this stack are the drain pipes from the various fixtures such as the sink, washbasin, shower, and toilet. The law of gravity being what it is and since we want the waste water to go down and out the drain, these pipes are connected to the upright pipe at a downward pitch. All fixtures are equipped with traps, those U-shaped pieces of pipe under sinks and the like, which hold enough water back to stop sewer gas from coming back up through the drains and sneaking into the house. Because of these traps, fumes must either stay where they are or escape through the vent in the roof.

Before we poured our floors, a length of 4-inch soil pipe with a clean-out entrance was run through the 6-inch opening left through the foundation in the corner of the shower (see chapter iv, "Foundation for the Adobe House"), and the stack was started. The clean-out is just outside the foundation wall and provides a place to start a reamer in case there is ever a serious stoppage. The toilet drain was connected directly to this stack with a "closet bend" and a short length of 4-inch cast iron pipe. The shower drain with its trap and the waste lines from the wash basin were connected to the stack with 1½-inch galvanized pipe and drainage fittings, the connection being made with a 4″ x 1½″ tapped tee. The basin was vented with a 1½-inch pipe passing straight up through the shower partition wall and through the roof.

The sink drainage system was made of 2-inch soil pipe running down and out under the porch. There is another clean-out on this line on a tee. A tee incidentally is a T-shaped pipe fitting. Others in the plumbing fitting alphabet are P, L, Y, U, and S bends. By using them singly or in combination, straight pieces of pipe may be made to go in any desired direction. The vent for our sink runs parallel to the wall behind the sink splashback, which conceals the supply pipes as well, and through a hole in the adobe partition wall between kitchen and bathroom and into the main stack. Except for the septic tank, which will be described later for the benefit of those whose buildings will not connect with city sewers, this completes the outline of the drainage system of our simple plumbing installation.

The clean-water supply is carried by ¾-inch galvanized water pipe from our well and enters the house through the bathroom wall above the foundation; it continues behind the shower and passes through the opening in the partition wall and goes behind the concealing splashback to the sink faucets. A branch pipe runs up and overhead behind the shower to connect to the hot-water supply. Pipes carrying hot and cold water to shower and lavatory also come down from above—through the hollow stud partition that forms one wall of the shower. Kitchen and bath are side by side, although separated by an adobe partition; thus confining our plumbing within a small area, we kept our pipe lines short and compact. (See chapter iii, p. 28, "Planning the Adobe House.") Our water is heated by means of coils in the wood stove in the kitchen which are connected to a storage tank close by.

Galvanized water pipe is connected by threads which screw into pipe couplings and other pipe fittings. Connections are always treated with a compound of some kind to make the joint water-tight. The compound is sometimes white lead, although there are numerous kinds and brands on the market. Obviously none of these connections should leak, and it is well to pay special attention to tightening the hot-water supply pipes since the heat will cause expansion and contraction at joints and make way for troublesome leaks.

The black-iron soil pipe comes in 5-foot lengths with one end expanded to a bell shape and the other straight. It is joined by inserting the straight end in a bell-shaped one and caulking and tamping the space left with oakum and hot lead. Oakum is made of hemp fibers that have been soaked in a tarry or oily substance. Caulking tools are shaped for tamping the oakum and lead in the circular space. When the joint is about two-thirds full of oakum which has been firmly tamped with the caulking tools and mallet or small hammer, the remaining space is poured full of melted lead. The lead is then forced down in the crack with the same tools. We joined as many of these iron pipe sections as we conveniently could while they could be held upright, since it is easier to do the caulking and lead pouring while they are in a vertical position. Unfortunately there comes a time when this is no longer possible. Then there is nothing to do but lay the pipes horizontally and go down on hands and knees and hang yourself headfirst in a ditch. After standing on your head pounding the oakum in, the asbestos joint runner is clamped around the pipe close to the joint and the molten lead is poured. That the lead stays in the crack all around the prone pipe always seems a minor miracle, but stay it does if the runner has been properly adjusted.

There should be a word of warning given here about the dangers of handling hot lead. Even though the building of your house is a family affair, see that the children stay well away from the lead pot. Wear gloves and don't breathe the fumes. Be very careful that no water gets near the hot lead as only a drop of cold water will cause it to spatter a long distance.

Plumbing being a backward affair, both supply and waste pipes are put in before the fixtures are set. This preparation for the setting of fixtures is known as "roughing-in." Before the roughing-in can begin, you must know the exact location of the fixtures, pipe sizes, and where the drain and supply pipes must come out of floors and walls. These rough-in dimensions vary in each style of fixture and there are many styles. Professional plumbers have catalogues of all the fixtures in the lines they use and in these catalogues are the rough-in dimensions for each fixture.

As already said, we selected our fixtures from the Sears catalogue for that season and received a chart with rough-ins for them clearly diagrammed. With this information we completed our plumbing plans.

It is likely that you have never considered how much water it takes to flush a toilet. We never had, but in studying our mail-order catalogue we perceived that different styles took varying amounts. As our water is supplied from a well in ordinarily sufficient amounts but not as inexhaustable as city water mains, we chose both toilet and shower head from those described as "water-savers." So far we have not flushed or showered our well dry. I could wish that among the lavatories there had been a number called an "easy-cleaner" or some-such, for the wash basin we chose has a space between mixing-faucet and wall that is a natural home for a bar of soap but is impossible to clean with anything but an old toothbrush. In choosing fixtures our advice would be to consider your water supply and how much time you want to spend cleaning them.

A properly designed septic tank is the solution to the problem of sewage disposal in rural homes that are equipped with plumbing and water-pressure systems. A cesspool, often found substituting for a septic tank, is a sorry makeshift, for it is dangerous and highly unsanitary. The system we built conforms to our county health code and is similar to the sewage-disposal systems recommended by the California State Department of Public Health, the University of Illinois Agricultural Experiment Station, and other authorities.

The principle on which the septic tank functions is the changing of solids into liquids by bacterial action. The bacteria working between the scum at the top of the tank and the silt in the bottom cause the liquefication. Thus there is only liquid to be finally disposed of at the

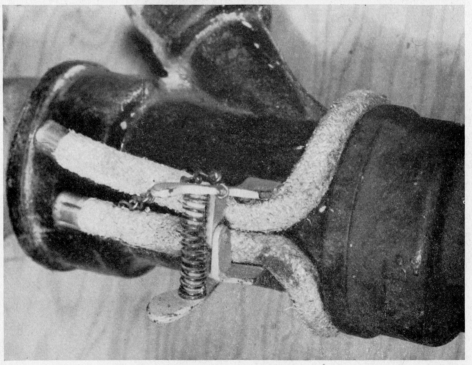

Asbestos joint runner in place on cast-iron soil-pipe fitting (LEFT). End of filter trench ready for earth back-fill, showing tile placed on boards over coarse gravel, tar paper strips over joints, more gravel and covering of tar paper (RIGHT).

tank's outlet. When it leaves the tank this effluent passes through sub-surface, open-jointed drain tile laid at a depth of 18 inches below ground and on a slight down grade away from the tank. The length of the discharge line depends on the porosity of the soil and the number of persons to be served by the system. Ordinarily 30 feet to 40 feet per person is needed. Our county ordinance requires a 100-foot minimum tile bed.

Before planning your sewage system it would be advisable to visit your county Board of Health and find out if a permit to install a septic tank is required and what, if any, are the specifications. In some in-stances an inspection of the installation must be made before it is covered. Requirements to be met and inspections made by officers of the health department are strictly for your own protection and do not come under the heading of red tape by any means.

Our septic tank is a two-compartment box made of poured concrete with walls 6 inches thick. Many tanks are only one-chamber, but the extra work and expense of the two-chamber box is justified by added efficiency of operation and the elimination of need for frequent cleaning and pumping of the tank. Fortunately a well-built septic tank will not need attention for years at a time.

The inside dimensions of the box are: width 3 feet, depth 5 feet. The large chamber on the inlet end is 6 feet long and the small chamber on the outlet end is 3 feet long (effective capacity 800 gallons). Baffle plates of 2-inch redwood were placed in both chambers. A reinforced concrete lid made in four sections, each section having double iron handles, was used for easy opening of the tank. The top of the tank is 18 inches below the surface of the ground.

The tank should be a minimum of 5 feet from the house and not more than 20 feet, the distance depending on existing conditions at the site, but the sewer lines should be short and straight. Neither sewer lines or tank should be close to wells, springs, or cisterns.

Gases formed in the tank will escape through the vents in the plumb-ing system of the house. Our tank is connected to the house sewer outlet with 4-inch cast-iron soil pipe. Concrete pipe may be used, but tree roots have a bad habit of seeking them out and growing disastrously in sewer lines where concrete pipe is used.

We had to pass a small well that we use for irrigation purposes with our sewer line, and due to this and other conditions in our layout we continued with cast-iron pipe on the outlet end of our septic tank for a distance of 30 feet. There it entered a small concrete distribution box, and from there we ran two tile lines, each one 50 feet long, and 6 feet apart. The long outlet and the distributing box are usually unnecessary, but a distributing box should be used where it is necessary to make a radical change in the direction of flow.

Now for a few construction details. First the whole system must be carefully planned and the layout and grades determined. The grade, or fall, from the house sewer outlet to the tank should not be less than 2 inches in 10 feet when using 4-inch pipe. If a line is to be run from the tank to a distributing box the downward grade should be uniform and not less than a half-inch in 10 feet. The fall in the trench filter, or tile bed line, is very slight, only 4 inches in 100 feet. Slow seepage, not flow, is desired in the tile bed so the flat angle is important.

Grades may be determined with a line and line level. To set the grade for the tile bed for example, drive a stout stake at the point where the tile bed is to start. Call that point *A*. Assuming that the length of the filter bed is to be 100 feet, drive stake *B* at that distance away. Attach a line to stake *A* and pull it tight and loop it around stake *B*. Hang a line level on the line or hold a regular level along it, shifting the line up and down at *B* until it is exactly level. Mark the level line on stake *B*. Now that you have the level line, the next step is to get the grade line. To do this measure down the number of inches of fall, in this case it should be 4 inches, from the level mark on stake *B*. Move string line down to the new mark and you have your grade line. Next cut a stick the depth of the proposed trench plus the distance to the cord above the ground at stake *A*. In our installation the trenches were 36 inches deep. The bottom of the trench excavation may be measured with this stick from the cord showing grade level. Other grades can be determined the same way.

When we dug the hole for the septic tank we found the soil firm (oh, how firm), and as it didn't tend to cave in we needed no outside forms for the concrete. We excavated to the exact dimensions of the tank and let the earth form the outside form. To keep the edges from breaking down, we outlined the hole with 2″ x 8″ planks nailed at the corners and set level. The planks also supported the inside wooden form when it was suspended in position.

With our previous experience in building foundation forms we found the forms for the tank easy to make. We built them above ground and lowered them into the hole. There were some tense moments while lowering them, and it took all hands and the cook, but we managed without mishap. A strong man, invited to help dig the hole, assisted at the form-lowering too. Incidentally here was a lot of earth for adobe brickmaking, but our bricks were all made and the house built by the time we put in the septic tank, so we carted it away and used it to fill up the "adobe mine."

Inlet and outlet pipes were placed in position through holes in the form made for them and the pouring of the concrete began. The mix was the same as that used for floors, a 1 to 2¼ to 3, with aggregate not larger than 1½ inches. It should be a stiff, not sloppy, mix and should be dumped evenly all around the sides and in the middle division, if there are two boxes to equalize the pressure against the form. Bring all side walls up for about 18 inches and then start filling in the bottom or floor. Some of the concrete will already have oozed in from the sides because there is no bottom in the form. Watch that the floor concrete does not rise higher than the bottom edges of the form or it will make removal of form boards difficult. When the floor is to height, continue pouring the walls until the top of the form is reached.

The lid sections were poured on a level surface; they were made large enough to rest across the top of the tank and were provided with handles for easy lifting. We found old horseshoes easy to stick in the concrete as it hardened; these made excellent handles. Each section was strengthened with reinforcing rod.

In building the tank we used 20 sacks of cement and 4¼ yards of concrete mix. Fifteen yards of gravel were used in the trench bed and 100 feet of 4-inch drain tile.

The filter trench calls for more digging and good strong backs. Our trenches were 36 inches deep, at least 12 inches below the septic tank outlet, and 24 inches wide. Grades were checked with line and stick. The bottom of the trench should be picked loose and covered with the crushed rock to a depth of 12 inches or more. This rock should be in 1-inch to 1½-inch pieces to allow a loose seepage bed. On top of the rock a 1″ x 4″ board is laid and on top of the board the line of tiles is placed. These tiles are arranged in a straight line with not less than a half-inch or more than a ¾-inch crack between them. Small pieces of rock wedged between them and the board will keep them from rolling out of line. The open joints are covered with 4-inch strips of tar paper. More gravel is then put over the tile, a couple of inches or so; care should be taken not to disturb the tar-paper joint covers. The next layer in the trench may be straw, burlap, or tar paper to keep loose dirt from sifting into the filter bed. We used strips of cheap tar paper. Before covering the tile we blocked the ends of the lines with a loose-fitting brick to keep curious moles and gophers out of the line. When the gravel was distributed over the tile and covered with the tar paper, the trenches were filled with dirt to original ground level. By that time the lids had cured enough to place over the tank, and when they were covered with soil our sewage system was complete.

References we found very helpful in this part of our job were Farmers' Bulletins 1572, *Making Cellars Dry;* 1772, *Use of Concrete on the Farm;* 1869, *Foundations for Farm Buildings;* 1227, *Sewage and Sewerage of Farm Homes;* 1426, *Farm Plumbing* and *Foundation Walls and Basements of Concrete* from the Portland Cement Association in Chicago, and the Sears, Roebuck & Company booklet, *Instructions for Installing Modern Plumbing Systems.*

VIII

Electric Wiring in the Adobe House

CANDLELIGHT on the texture of adobe walls is delightful, but if electricity is available at your building site you will want electric light besides. We did our own electric wiring and think that it is possible for even the inexperienced person to do a safe and acceptable job if certain rules are followed. It is true that this is a subject requiring study, particularly if all one knows about it to date is how to plug in a toaster or press a light switch!

As in other building operations, the adobe house presents some special problems when it comes time to consider wiring if for electricity. To begin with you should decide on the location and number of electrical convenience outlets and the lighting fixtures and appliances to be served; these should be included in the drawings of the house plans. We made a special wiring plan. While planning don't be stingy with outlets; have enough to serve all the appliances you now own and some to spare.

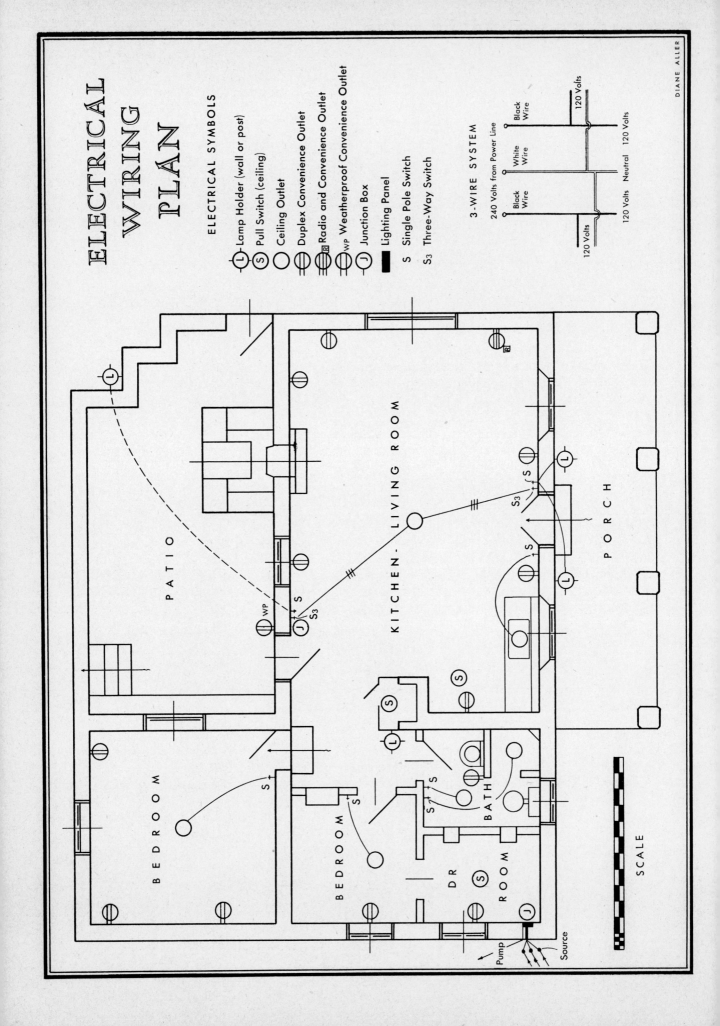

Also give thought to the location of light switches. They should be at your fingertips on entering a room, not behind a door or on the opposite wall. Noiseless switches will help preserve the natural quiet of the adobe house.

Service provided by power companies varies as do local codes and restrictions in different parts of the country, so it is impossible to be specific regarding the wiring for your house. Still, after a brief outline of wiring in general we can tell you how we wired our house.

In general the wiring system of a house includes all electrical conductors (wires) from the point of delivery to each outlet or device which utilizes electric power. Where a power company furnishes electricity, the point of delivery is known as the "service entrance." Here the main service wires connect to the meter and service box. The box usually contains the main switch and fuses and other fuse blocks for the branch circuits. From this service box small capacity wires called "branch circuits" deliver the electrical energy to lamps, convenience outlets, and appliances. There are from four to six branch circuits in the average house.

On each branch circuit a fuse or fuses are installed to protect the system from overloading or from short-circuit currents. This device works automatically in case of trouble and disconnects the circuit by the melting of a link or wire made of a low-melting-point alloy. Small capacity fuses enclosed in a porcelain cup are known as "plug fuses;" larger capacity fuses are enclosed in a fiber tube and are called "cartridge fuses." A circuit breaker is a more modern device that performs the same duties as a fuse but is reset simply by tripping a handle, thus requiring no replacements as do blown fuses.

The standard branch circuit for general lighting use is a 15-ampere circuit which is protected by a 15-ampere fuse. The wires for a 15-ampere circuit should not be smaller than No. 14. The circuit used for average home appliances (not including ranges, water heaters, or large room-heaters) is a 20-ampere circuit requiring 20-ampere fuses. No. 12 wire is usually required for these branch circuits.

While there are seven types of wiring used in houses, we shall only consider the four most often employed. They are: conduit, both rigid and thin-wall; flexible steel-armored cable; flexible non-metallic sheathed cable; and either concealed or open knob and tube.

Conduit is a metal casing similar to pipe but smooth inside and heavily coated with a rust-proof finish of enamel or galvanized material. Rigid conduit is cut and threaded like water pipe and connected to boxes, etc., with bushings and lock-nuts. In spite of the apparent similarity, water or gas pipe should not be substituted for rigid conduit. Thin-wall conduit is joined with special connectors without threading. Insulated wires are pulled through these metal casings.

In flexible steel-armored cable, insulated wires are protected by a winding of sheet metal strips. It is commonly called "BX" cable.

Multiple wrappings of laminated kraft tape and cotton braids impregnated with a moisture-resistant compound protect the wires of the flexible non-metallic sheathed cable.

Insulated, but otherwise unprotected, individual wires are supported on porcelain knobs in the knob-and-tube system. Porcelain tubes protect the wire where it passes through parts of the structure (joists, rafters, etc.).

While electric power is transmitted and distributed by both direct current (D.C.) and alternating current (A.C.), most of the electric power for homes is transmitted by alternating current. This is because alternating current transmits power economically at high voltages for long distances and because voltages may be raised or lowered through transformers at either or both ends of the line.

A.C. distribution for small buildings is usually accomplished by means of a single-phase two-wire system carrying 110 volts or a three-wire system of 220 volts. The two-wire system consists of one wire carrying 110 volts and the other a neutral or grounded wire. The three-wire system has two outer wires each carrying 110 volts and a center neutral or grounded wire. By adding the volts in the two outer wires of this system we have a potential of 220 volts. Ranges and other heavy-duty appliances require the 220-volt system; 110 volts is sufficient for light and small appliances. Going back to the two-wire or three-wire systems, by using one outer wire and a connection from it to the center neutral wire, a 110-volt line is obtained for ordinary use. Thus a three-wire system is essentially two two-wire circuits in which the neutral wires are combined and made common to the two circuits.

In electrical work, as in any other, it is important to know the meaning of some of the common terms used. "Volts," for instance, measure electric pressure or amount of electromotive force; in other words, how much "juice" is available to your house. "Amperes" are measures of the quantity of current flowing in a circuit, while "watts" is the product obtained by multiplying the number of volts by the number of amperes. Appliances are often rated in watts; you may find how much current it uses (rating in amperes) by dividing the number of watts by the number of volts you have. "Circuits" are the power-carrying branches of the electrical system.

In planning your electrical system the number of circuits you will need must be determined so that adequate wiring and fusing is provided. Here is a formula for finding the number of circuits needed: figure area in square feet of floor space of all areas to be used for living purposes. Multiply by two (this is the minimum wattage required). Add to this minimum the total appliance load (irons, toasters, portable heaters, etc.), also figured in watts. Divide this figure by the number of volts— 110, 220, or whatever your power in volts. The answer is the approximate number of amperes you will need. As 15 amperes is the maximum number permitted on most circuits (appliance circuits carry 20 amperes), divide the total number of amperes required by 15 to find the number of circuits required. This may not come out even but for a trouble-free system don't overload circuits. A 20-ampere appliance circuit should be included in the total number of circuits.

Most electrical appliances are rated according to the number of watts they use, as are light globes, so it is not hard to estimate the wattage you will use if number and kind of lighting fixtures and appliances are known. Generally, circuits are designed to carry an estimated load of 1,200 watts, and this is the limit allowed in many localities. Frequently it is further stipulated that no branch circuit have more than twelve outlets. The maximum load for No. 14 wire is 110 volts, 15 amperes, and 1,650 watts.

Independent circuits are usually installed for the following devices or groups of devices: oil burners, electric ranges, lights and outlets for washing machine and mangle in the laundry room, workshop lights and outlets for power-driven tools, refrigerator, heating appliances drawing more than 1000 watts, and for any apparatus with a motor larger than ¼ horsepower.

If you have read this far without being electrocuted, congratulations!

If you are still with us but in a daze, take heart, for we too were not always so knowing. Time was when "watt" was just a word printed on light globes as far as we were concerned. We weren't much farther along in electrical knowledge when we received a detailed booklet on wiring included in a shipment of wiring materials ordered from Sears, Roebuck & Company. It was most helpful. Grounding, polarizing, and all kinds of connections were plainly pictured and diagrammed in this booklet, which was planned to take the customer on an electrician's tour of what seemed to be a haunted house, judging from the illustrations. After following circuit after circuit on page after page through this extensive building, we gained confidence in our ability to wire our own simple dwelling. However, as the requirements for wiring an adobe differ from those given in the best of wiring instructions, most of them dealing exclusively with frame construction, we had best get back to the adobe.

The power company which serves our house supplies alternating-current three-wire 240-volt service, instead of the usual 220-voltage. The company installs lines up to the house but from that point the service connections, lines to meter and to switch and fuse boxes, are installed by the householder. Our power line comes onto the garage roof at the minimum allowed height of 10 feet above ground, the garage being closer to the power line than the house. It is secured to the edge of the roof with heavy insulators. From there the power is carried through a service-entrance cap and service-entrance cable to the meter on an outside wall. This service-entrance cable is a heavy, waterproof cable containing two No. 6 gauge insulated wires and one bare, stranded No. 6 gauge copper wire. In the three-wire system, the bare wire is neutral and is grounded near the meter.

The local code will usually specify the type of service entrance required. In some localities rigid conduit will be called for. Conduit 1 inch in diameter will hold three No. 8 wires; conduit ¾ inch in diameter will hold two No. 8 wires. For three No. 6 wires, conduit 1¼ inches in diameter will be needed.

The service-entrance cable passes through the meter, turning to go through a hole in the adobe wall of the garage to the main switch and fuses inside. Where conduit is required, an entrance ell may be used to make the turn, although conduit may be bent as long as the radius of the curve it is shaped to is not less than six times the diameter of the conduit used.

One of the problems in wiring an adobe is keeping the wiring out of sight, for there are no conveniently hollow walls to hide it in as there are in frame houses. To conceal the wiring inside our adobe we ran some of it through conduit in the foundation and inside the brick walls. We used non-metallic cable where we could put it inside stud partitions and overhead on top of the living-room beams and along the top of the collar beam.

Some day, by means of underground "parkway" cable, we will conceal the outside wires that bring the current from garage to house but at present they are simply strung overhead. When they reach the house from the garage, these three No. 8 wires go through a service cap on 1-inch conduit which runs a few feet down the outside of the house wall before it turns and goes through the brick wall to a flush cabinet holding the switches and fuses. Again the neutral wire is grounded on the outside of the house.

Now for a description of the conduit work: the cabinet mentioned above, a $9\frac{3}{4}''$ x $6\frac{3}{4}''$ box, holds a switch and main fuses of 30 amperes as well as four single-fused circuit branches. The shell of the cabinet was cast in concrete in position on the dressing room wall as it was erected. A threaded piece of 1-inch conduit was passed through a "knock-out" (a circular scoring in the metal, easily removable and leaving a round hole) in the back of the cabinet and connected to the entrance ell coming through the wall. Conduit was run through another knock-out in the bottom of the switch cabinet, down to the top of the foundation, and from the top of the cabinet up through the collar beam for overhead wires. The $\frac{3}{4}$-inch conduit going from the bottom of the box was partly sunk in a 1-inch groove, largest allowed in a 12-inch adobe wall, and continued down to the top of the foundation where it was connected to a 4-inch square, outlet junction box which had been imbedded in the concrete. The opening of this junction box was flush with the inside of the foundation wall. Half-inch conduit went from knock-outs at both ends of this box to extend around the foundation. Where floor-level convenience outlets were desired, deep utility boxes were put in. Conduit and boxes were installed before the foundation was poured. (See chapter iv, "Foundation for the Adobe House," p. 40.)

The ¾-inch conduit leaving the top of the switch and fuse cabinet was also let in part way in a 1-inch chase cut in the wall and was continued up through the bond beam for a couple of inches where it entered another 4-inch-square junction box. This pipe was installed after the wall was up and before the bond beam was poured.

Light switches and wall outlets were placed in position as the walls were built. Switches were set approximately 48″ from the floor but this distance may vary to suit the brick courses and personal preferences. As has been said elsewhere, these were contained in deep-type boxes. Switch boxes were set singly, in pairs, or in threes as needed. Conduit was connected to the rear of the boxes and bent to run parallel with the wall to the back of the near-by door jamb. There it was bent again to run up to the collar beam. To avoid fitting bricks around these bends, the whole section, one brick deep and full wall thickness, was cast in concrete. (See chapter v, "Laying the Walls of the Adobe House," p. 51.) Factory-bent elbows are available and should be a convenience. If you bend the conduit, remember that half-inch conduit must not be bent to form a curve with a radius of less than 3 inches; 1-inch conduit must not be bent to less than a 6-inch radius.

All of this conduit work must be done during the construction of the foundation and walls. Conduit going to the top of the wall should project through the collar beam for at least 2 inches to clear the roof plate and should be set in from the inside wall about 3 inches.

For the sake of literary continuity, we will say that after our conduit and switch and outlet boxes were all in, the next step was to bring the three No. 8 outside wires in from the main service switch box on the garage and connect them to the house switch cabinet. Actually this was not done until after the house wiring was in and tested.

Keep in mind that the two outside wires of the three carry 110 volts apiece and that the center is the neutral or ground wire. Naturally you will not be working with any of them while current runs through them. We will call the outside "hot" wires the "black wires" and the center neutral wire the "white wire." For inside work you may use black and white-coated wire this way and it simplifies procedure. Colored wire is not used outside.

The two black wires from the house service entrance pass through the double pole switch and the main fuses and connect to the branch-circuit fuses. Our house has four of these branch-circuit fuses. One of them runs outside to the pump house to supply current for our new electric pump and the other three serve floor convenience outlets, overhead lights, and wall outlets in kitchen area and bathroom.

The white wire is connected to a bus bar on the bottom of the switch cabinet and all white wires throughout the system connect to it. From this bar a wire runs to the grounding pipe which extends 8 feet into the ground (should extend to a level where the ground is always damp), where the wire is clamped to it with a special grounding connection. Another special connection, a grounding bushing (sometimes called a bonding bushing), is used where the conduit enters the fuse cabinet and wire is connected to it from this bushing to the white connection on the box. Thus all the white wires are grounded and the whole length of conduit as well. This grounding of conduit and boxes is a matter of safety as it will automatically cause a fuse to blow should a live wire accidentally touch exposed metal; this prevents dangerous shocks and possible fires. Of course there is no fire hazard within the adobe walls themselves, but other points in the system may be vulnerable and it is only good sense to take precautions. Individual runs of conduit in the walls are grounded by connecting them to water-supply pipes.

After leaving the switch and fuse cabinet, a black and a white wire were drawn through the conduit going from the bottom of the cabinet and connecting through the junction box to the duplex outlets at the floor level. The black wire goes to the brass screw on the duplex outlet and the white wire to the white, actually nickel-plated, screw. Splices should never be made in the wire where they would occur inside the conduit. Wires for the overhead wiring passed out through the top of the cabinet, into the conduit, to the junction box at the top of the wall, and thence by non-metallic cable along wall plates or over closed ceilings to the various points above wall height.

Where wires went from wall switches beside the doors to overhead lights they did so through short lengths of conduit in the wall from the switch boxes to the top of the wall where they entered junction boxes. Non-metallic cable was affixed to these overhead boxes with special connectors made for non-metallic cable. The wire joints were soldered and taped with both rubber and black friction tape, and the boxes were covered with blank plates. While on the subject of soldering it might be well to say that paste is used when soldering electric wire, but acid or acid-core solder is never used in this work.

For easy identification we used a black and a white wire for the duplex outlet boxes, black wire only on one-way switches and red, white, and black wire on three-way switches. Anticipating heavy loads on our system (photographic lights, power tools, etc.) we used No. 12 wire throughout the house. This gauge is ordinarily used only on appliance circuits, No. 14 being considered sufficiently heavy for lighting circuits.

Outlet boxes and wall-switch boxes in the stud partitions must be set out from the studs to the thickness of the wall-covering you plan to use so they will be flush with the finished wall. We used a half-inch fiberboard on our few stud partitions so the boxes extended a half-inch beyond the 2″ x 4″ studs. Boxes in these partition walls were wired with non-metallic cable and connectors. Outlet boxes were also placed for the overhead lights, and both boxes and wiring were concealed in false beams or above ceilings in those rooms which are ceiled.

Tools you will need to do your own wiring are: a hack saw for cutting conduit, and a pipe stock and dies for threading it, pipe wrenches, pipe bender (see chapter iv, "Foundation for the Adobe House," p. 41), a steel tape for pulling wires through conduit, automobile or gas pliers, electrician's or linesman's pliers, a pair of long round-nosed pliers for making loops, a knife, screwdriver, soldering iron or small torch for soldering connections, and a test lamp.

A test lamp is a light globe in a composition socket with short wires connected to and extending from it. The ends of these wires are bare. In testing, the bare ends are held to touch corresponding wires in switches, etc. If juice is coming through to these connections, the globe will light up.

When all our outlets and switches were wired but before the joints were soldered and taped, the whole system was checked and tested with the test lamp to see that all was in order. Then the wire connections were soldered and taped and the box covers screwed in place. Ends of wires that were to go to fixtures not yet made were wrapped with tape and left for the time. With the exception of installing these fixtures, another phase of our housebuilding was finished.

IX

Finishing the Adobe House

EVEN with the big jobs done there was still much to do before our house was finished. Many of our week ends were filled with the smaller projects—laying floor tiles, hanging doors and windows, framing and finishing inside partitions, staining, painting, and whitewashing.

Painting the exterior is one of the biggest finishing jobs, one of the most expensive, and a very important part of finishing a frame house—important because it preserves wood from the ravages of weather; a wood surface must have the protection of several coats of good paint. Waterproofed adobe does not need this kind of protection, so it can be left as is or coated with whitewash or any kind of paint that will adhere to a non-absorbent surface. Because it was cheap and easy to handle and the cost of upkeep was negligible, plus the fact that we liked the effect, we used whitewash made of nothing but unslaked lime and cold water.

91

Because we wanted an off-white for the inside walls and have never come across a formula for coloring whitewash, we used one of the powdered casein paints mixed with cold water; these paints do not flake or rub off. Before the inside walls were painted they were gone over with a large, coarse scrubbing brush to knock off any loose dirt or mortar. We have been asked many times if adobe walls can be plastered. We understand that they will hold plaster very well if the cracks between the bricks are left unchinked. Undoubtedly a smooth plaster wall would make a more finished house and many would prefer it. We didn't even consider it, for what may seem a silly reason, and that is because I am given to driving nails in walls to hang things on (a number of landlords still hate me), and driving nails in plaster is very bad for the plaster. I can drive nails in my adobe walls to my heart's content. As it is, we like the brick texture inside the house just as well as we do outside.

My active dislike for certain phases of housekeeping influenced many interior details. There is no painted woodwork, for instance. Although I will spend hours polishing a copper pot, I loathe washing painted woodwork, so in my adobe house I resolved that there would be none to wash. It is all redwood, stained with a mixture of powdered burnt umber and boiled linseed oil. I might go over it with more oil some day but so far I haven't done anything to it.

Keeping the ordinary floor in shape is not my idea of a good time either. We laid tile floors throughout the house and find them satisfactory from every standpoint. They are a little hard on anything you might drop, especially if it is fragile, sometimes if it is not. I broke a cast-iron frying pan by dropping it on the tile and iron frying pans aren't considered fragile. It didn't hurt the floor any though, and neither does anything else. Gritty dirt tracked in from the garden, which would cut the surface of the finest linoleum or hardwood, only polishes our tile. Wear only enhances it and it is hard to imagine that it would ever wear out and need replacing. Better housekeepers than I have asked me if the tiles couldn't be waxed and polished. Of course they can be, but mine won't be. Not by me.

These are the baked terra-cotta tile, sometimes called "patio" tile, not the expensive quarried ones; they are somewhat irregular but any irregularities in either the tile or their laying suit the casual, carefree spirit of the rest of the house. In the smaller rooms we used the 8″ x 8″

size. In the large main room we used 12-inch squares. There are many sizes made in this type of tile. Our large tile came in the form of regular hollow building tile which was scored so it could be broken into separate parts. By giving the whole tile an oblique rap at one corner on hard ground or on a log, it collasped into two 12-inch squares and two narrow side and center strips. We used the strips in a basket weave pattern on the porch floor and in walks.

We started the tile-laying on our little bedroom floor, first mopping the cleaned concrete slab with hot tar. This was a messy job and one we abandoned then and there. On the other floors we laid heavy tar paper with overlapping seams for a moisture stop. We could have used a waterproofed mortar and dispensed with the tar paper.

As it was we used mortar made of one part cement to four parts of sand, covering a few feet of floor at a time to a depth of a half-inch, using half-inch screed strips to mark off the sections and to level the mortar. The tiles were first soaked in water and then placed two or three at a time, leveled, and set by putting a short length of two-by-four across them and giving it several sharp raps with a hammer. The general level should be checked from time to time with a long mason's level.

The larger tiles were set a half-inch apart on all sides; $\frac{3}{8}$ inch was the allowance between the smaller tiles. Since the tiles are not perfectly square or flat, a little compromise is in order, but the general effect should be as level and even as you can make it. Some of the mortar will be forced up in the cracks when the tile is set, but it should not be so wet as to run over the tops.

When a section is complete from wall to wall, the screed strips should be removed and another section outlined. Before the setting bed of mortar hardens but is set up a bit, the cracks between the tile are filled with a creamy mixture, a "grout" made of one part cement to two parts of sand. This is poured in the cracks; any that gets on the surface of the tile may be wiped off with newspaper or rags. A fine film of concrete may adhere to parts of the surface but it soon wears off in use, or the tile may be cleaned later with a weak solution of muriatic acid.

Another way to fill the cracks is to mix damp sand together with cement and sweep it around on the floor until the cracks are packed with it. Any surplus can be swept away. This is easier than using the grout but it leaves a rougher, more porous finish.

Where it is necessary, tiles may be cut by scoring them with a sharp cold chisel and a hammer and breaking them along the score mark.

We gave our floors an oiled finish by mopping a heavy coat of used crankcase oil which had been strained through several layers of cheese-cloth. The oil was allowed to soak into the tile surface which was then given a rub-down with old gunny sacks. Without the oil treatment they would have shown grease spots, for the tile is porous.

Ceramic, or glazed, tiles are also soaked in water for a time before they are set in the mortar and tapped level with a rubber hammer or an ordinary one if the face of the tile is shielded by a piece of board. Diane used a mixture of fine sand and cement (one part cement and ap-proximately three parts sand) to set them in and filled the cracks with a grout of sifted sand and about an equal amount of cement. Experi-menting with white cement for the setting of the tile in the window sills, she decided that it set too rapidly and that the white color of the cracks diluted and weakened the rich colors of the tile. In her opinion the regular gray mortar made of common cement was not only better to work with but gave a better effect. Where tile was set in a vertical position against a wall she found the safest course was to brace a board against the tile until the mortar hardened. Admitting that this may be unprofessional, it did prevent disappointing accidents.

We tiled our sinkboard and the splashback above it, too. Paul built the cabinets first. Doors and drawers were made of ¾-inch plywood, the top of redwood. A layer of heavy tar paper was fitted over the boards making the sink top and the splashback. Galvanized mesh was tacked over the paper and then a half-inch layer of mortar was plastered over the wire. Tiles were set about one-eighth inch apart.

The tile mosaic that gave Diane many pleasant hours was made by breaking and fitting small scraps of tile to form a picture or design of her fancy. The pieces of tile were fitted together much as a jig-saw puzzle is put together, except that a narrow crack is allowed between each piece for mortar. The pattern is first drawn to size on a piece of heavy wrapping paper; then the bits of tile are stuck in place, color side up, with ordinary flour paste made by cooking a little flour and water together. Large mosaics are made in joining sections but smaller ones may be completed on one piece of paper in a single unit. When the design is completed and pasted to the first paper, the entire surface of the mosaic is covered with a water-soluble paste and another piece of stout paper or light cloth is pasted over it. When the paste is dry, the mosaic is turned over, bottom side up, and the first paper backing is soaked off. Care must be taken not to loosen the pieces from the top paper or cloth. A level bed of mortar is spread on the surface to receive the mosaic, which is turned right side up again and the under side lowered into the mortar. Before the protecting cover is removed, the many small pieces of tile are tapped level and pressed into the mortar under a short length of board. Moisture from the mortar which will have seeped up through the cracks will have wet the cloth or paper and dissolved the paste sufficiently to remove it. Unfilled cracks are then filled with fine grout and the surface wiped gleamingly clean. Diane's only tools for breaking the tile to size and shape were a small hammer and a couple of cold chisels.

One of the next steps in the house finishing was to hang the doors and windows. Two of our windows are large steel ones purchased from a wrecking yard in the city. They were purchased early, before the house was started, and we made openings in the walls to fit them. The rest of the windows are casements of a standard mill size, hung to swing in rather than out, and all of our windows are placed at the outer edge of the walls to give us wide sills and deep reveals inside.

Our doors, both exterior and interior, we made ourselves. The exterior doors are made of 2″ x 6″ redwood planks, put together with dowels and resin glue. The front door is a double one, hung in a 4-foot opening. The inside doors, made later, are paneled in a diagonal pattern. I don't know how the back door escaped adornment, all the others are carved.

The work of finishing was made easier by the acquisition of several power tools. Our guesthouse, built first, was made entirely with hand tools but we later bought an 8-inch circular saw, a drill press, a portable electric drill, a jointer, and a small band saw; all of these were a big help on the main house. As power tools go, ours are medium-sized but did a lot of big jobs.

To get back to the hanging of the doors and windows, we'll start with the large steel windows which, properly speaking, weren't hung at all but set solidly to look out on the weather side of the house. First a strip of molding was nailed to the wooden frames at the sides close to the

Angled bricks were cast for windows with flared sides. All windows were placed at the outer edge of the walls to give wide window sills and deep reveals.

outside edge. Next the inner surface of the molding was well buttered with mastic, a sticky waterproof compound, and the window was pressed against it. Strips were then cut to fit under the angle-iron bottom edge of the window, smeared with more mastic, and toenailed in place. A finishing piece of quarter-round molding was tacked around the outside. The wooden window frames were nailed to nailing blocks which were put in place when the sill was poured. Had we overlooked the nailing blocks, there are special anchor shields and fasteners to go into concrete and holes for them can be made with a star drill and hammer, but preplanned nailing blocks are simpler.

The sides of two of our windows flare out—specially-made angled bricks form the flare—and on these a 1″ x 3″ wooden strip was nailed at top and bottom. The hinges were affixed to the 2″ x 4″ frames at the sides. All the other window frames are 2″ x 12″ and on these the 1″ x 3″ strips were nailed completely around the frame.

In hanging double casement windows it is best to work from a center plumb line as the sides may not be exactly square. By nailing the stop around the outside (for windows that open in), one may fit the casements and hold them in place with wooden wedges while marking the location of the 2-inch loose-pin butt hinges. Allow from $\frac{1}{16}$ to $\frac{1}{8}$ inch clearance all around. The mortises for the hinges are carefully marked with a sharp knife point on both the jambs and the stiles and then are cut out with a chisel until the hinge leaf fits flush. Fit one part of the window first and fit the other half to it. Our casements are closed with regular casement bolts at the top for practical purposes but have wrought-iron curlicue fasteners at the near center because we like their looks.

Doors are always made oversize so they may be cut to fit when they are hung. On single doors, trim the bottom square and then stand it on $\frac{3}{8}$-inch blocks for clearance allowance and hold it up against the jamb on the inside face. Have an assistant on the other side mark around the inside of the jamb onto the door. When the door is sawed or planed to these marks it should fit with sufficient clearance on top, sides, and bottom.

Nail temporary stops around the door jambs so the door will come flush with the inside wall when it is held against the stops. Put the $\frac{3}{8}$-inch blocks under it again and place it in position. Drive two wedges in the crack on the lock side so the door is forced and held against the hinge side of the jamb. We used three 4-inch butt hinges for these heavy doors. To put on the hinges, make a mark 6 inches down on both casing and door to locate the top of the top hinge. Measuring up from the floor, make another mark on door and casing at 10 inches above the floor. The 10-inch mark from the floor marks the place for the lower edge of the bottom hinge. The third hinge is centered between the top and bottom hinges.

Take the door down again and mark around the hinges for the mortises, or "gains" as they are sometimes called, on both the door and the jamb. Don't let the hinge come clear to the outside edge of the door—hold it back ¼ inch, that is leave ¼ inch of wood beyond the edge of the hinge leaf. The mortises are cut with wood chisels to a depth allowing the hinge to set in flush with the door surface.

The loose pins are drawn and the leaves screwed in place on the casing and the door, after which the door is put back in place, fitting knuckles of the hinges, and the pins are replaced. If the marking and cutting has been done with accuracy the door should swing freely. If it binds, the trouble may be corrected by loosening one of the leaves and putting a cardboard shim under it, or it may be that one of the mortises should be slightly deepened. Only by experimenting will the exact cause of the trouble be found. If the two jambs are not in line, the door may not be in perfect alignment with the jamb on the lock side. In this case one of the hinges on the jamb should be moved out as needed. It is best to make a trial before all the screws are set. When the door fits to your satisfaction door stops are nailed around the opening. We used ⅞″ x 3″ molding, ripped from roof sheathing remnants.

Our front door, being a double one, had one side fitted first and then the other was fitted to it as with the casement windows. Be sure to check the jambs on a double door. If they are not true the doors will not meet at the center, and it will be necessary to move hinges back and forth until the door edges do meet properly. To close the crack between the doors we nailed and glued a strip of carved hardwood to the door that opens first. A hand-wrought iron bolt was put at the top of the other door. We have ornamental iron knockers on the two doors but no conventional latches or locks. A large button catch at the top of the door that opens first holds it closed, and a hand-wrought heavy iron bar bolts the doors shut on the inside. A regular Yale lock is fitted on the back door which also has a handmade latch. Felt weather stripping was put at the lower edge of both outside doors.

We could now lock up our house when we had to leave it on Sunday nights and needn't put things away so carefully.

Our next project was erecting the inside partitions. The shoe or floor plates were already in, for they were installed on the bolts left for them in the concrete before the tiles were laid. The upright studs were nailed to the floor plates. Where they came alongside adobe walls they were bolted to the adobe with bolts set in holes drilled in the adobe and filled with mortar around the bolt. Double studs were used at the door openings and in corners. Also in the corners were nailing strips for the wall board. Openings for the built-in shelves in the bathroom and closet and the linen closet in the hallway were framed. Next ceiling joists were placed, and wall plate on top of the studs, and the wall plate on the bond beam. The shower walls were also framed and covered with metal lath for plastering.

After the framing was up, but before it was covered with wallboard, all wiring and plumbing that went inside the partitions was completed to the point of installing the fixtures. We did connect a few of the floor outlet plugs for convenience in using the electric saw, etc.

One of the next steps was to box the ridgeboard to make it look like a solid beam. It is really only a square trough with mitered edges cut to a 45-degree angle and nailed and glued together. This trough was held below the ridgeboard against the rafters to mark notches, which when cut slipped over the rafters and snug against the roof. The "beam" was fastened to the ridgeplate with lag screws. More hollow beams, made square and with mitered edges were placed upright on our genuine, solid crossbeams at the room center to run up to meet the ridge beam. These uprights concealed overhead electric wiring in our main room.

After that was done the open gable ends were framed with odds and ends of 2″ x 4″ for the wallboard there. It was marked, cut, and nailed up before the side pieces were put on. Covering the space along the side walls between the top of the bond beam and the underside of the roof is tricky. This is the way we did it. Short pieces of 1″ x 3″ lumber, top ends cut to the roof angle, were nailed to each side of each rafter and were long enough to reach from the roof sheathing to the top of the bond beam. Across the faces of these pieces 1″ x 2″ strips were nailed.

Interior room doors are carved and panelled in a diagonal pattern. The small door is of cleated vertical boards with turned spindles in ventilating opening.

At the top of the gap the pieces were just long enough to go between the rafters; at the bottom long strips were used. They were set back a half-inch so that the wallboard would come flush with the rest of the wall when it was nailed to them. Long strips of the wallboard were held up against the line of rafters and marked so the wallboard could be cut out to fit around them. The top edges of the wallboard were slightly beveled with coarse sandpaper to conform to the roof slope, making a close fit there.

Follow the instructions given by the makers of your particular board, if you use it, but don't get the joints too close. We allowed about a quarter inch and filled the cracks with the recommended crack filler and sanded it slightly.

When the walls were painted and the wallboard was painted the same off-white, we gazed up at the brown-stained roof sheathing and beams and our off-white walls and realized with a shock that we had a very neat effect, but it was on the order of the English half-timbered houses. In any event it wasn't Mexican, nor was it Aller; I got on a ladder and proceeded to bring it in line. Using motifs taken from the original decorations on Aztec manuscript and lots of bright colors I painted flowering vines along the wallboard strip under the rafters and birds and animals and even Quetzalcoatl, the principal god of the Aztecs, on the wallboard in the gable ends. I had a wonderful time doing it, even if I did bring Diane to the verge of a nervous breakdown. She feared that in my absorption I would attempt to stand back and view my artistry while on a ladder and land flat on the tile below! I didn't, and the painted panels around the top of the room are extremely decorative.

Before the wallboard was put on the frame partition walls, the door frames of 4″ x 6″ carved redwood were bolted to the studs with carriage bolts.

One of the last of the finishing jobs was to install the plumbing fixtures according to the directions which came with them and plaster the shower. It was in plastering the 3′ x 3′ ceiling that Paul nearly had his first housebuilding failure. Three times he got it covered with the plaster and three times it fell down on his unbowed head. The fourth time it stayed put.

On one Fourth of July we had poured the foundation of our adobe house. By Thanksgiving the last brick was laid and by the next Fourth of July we had moved in. Not a record-breaking speed for housebuilding, but the actual working time would be hard to determine as it was all done on week ends and during two short summer vacations—two-week ones. Had it taken longer, we wouldn't have minded for we enjoyed every minute of it.

True, there were times when we were weary and perplexed by some particular housebuilding complexity, but when it was worked out satisfactorily, we rejoiced and tackled the next step. We were wholehearted in our concentration on each phase of the construction, and when it was complete we were better prepared to cope with the following one and any troubles were quickly forgotten except as experience gained.

X

Owning the Adobe House

As WE COME to this last chapter, a short dissertation on the desirability of owning an adobe house, let us remark that many people are anxious to own any kind of a house and are being balked in these desires by material shortages. Shortages threaten to get worse before they get better. During the war years thousands of men and women promised themselves a reward for sacrifices made then, and in many instances the reward was to be a home. No wonder that the current of dissatisfaction caused by the frustration of those plans is strong. The war is over but a hundred reasons still exist to explain why all of these home-hungry ones cannot have their dreams fulfilled at once. Although they may not move into a finished house right away, some of them can escape the gnawing frustration of doing nothing but waiting for that day when materials and skilled manpower are plentiful. *You* can.

"You and your husband hold a country home in your own four hands

103

Lamp and gate on zigzag wall add interest to a corner of the patio.

today—if you want to use them. And you can build it for almost nothing if you charge the material costs against recreation and keep the enterprise on a strictly let's-make-it-fun basis."

Those words, written by Gilbert Stanley Underwood, Supervising Architect, Public Buildings Administration, were published in a nationally distributed magazine only a few months ago. We were glad to read them, for one of the greatest pleasures in being able to read is finding, in print, confirmation of one's own pet ideas. The writer's suggestion that the young couple or family take their fun time and fun money and build themselves a home is just what we have been preaching, as well as practicing. We are also in agreement when he says that the best way to get a house that will really suit you is to build it with your own hands. The main thing, says Mr. Underwood, is to look around for a suitable location for your combined picnic-building excursions, note what materials are the most plentiful, and begin.

Unfortunately, a list of the materials that are not plentiful would, at present, be much longer than a list of those that are. Much of the earth in our land is no longer cheap, but there is as much of it as there ever was. By now you will have gathered that adobe bricks are made of earth and that they may be made of practically any earth, any place throughout the length and breadth of the land. Adobe shouldn't be thought of as a substitute for any type of building material, however. Adobe bricks will make a good house, one that will compete with one made of any material, no matter how plentiful or how scarce it may be. Best of all, for the person who would do the work himself in hours after the day's or week's wage-earning stint is through, is the fact that adobe building lends itself to any speed.

Mr. Underwood suggests that a fireplace, preferably a double one for inside and outside use, be built the first summer. This seems a very good idea, but an ambitious family could make some adobe bricks as well. We made all of ours in the free time during one summer. If a fireplace was built first for later incorporation into an adobe house, lengths of reinforcing rod should be built into the structure and left protruding far enough to fasten firmly in the wall to be built later. It could be bent back out of the way until then.

If you plan to build with adobe one room at a time, building on to them later, those side walls or partitions to be extended should be left with bricks staggered at the ends for later bricks to fit to. Loops of the barbed wire which runs through every sixth course should be left long enough to make an 18-inch overlap with the new start of wire, and rods could extend from the collar beam as well.

In our experience, however, we found that building all of the brick walls at once was not too difficult or too expensive. Of course the roof and the foundation are the biggest items from a financial point of view, but if they could be managed, much of the inside finishing could wait for more time or money. Built-ins, partitions, tiling or other final finishing of floors, inside doors, painting of either interior or exterior—all these could wait. We found that it took a certain amount of time to use up purchased material and that while we were working on that we were collecting a few more dollars as we went along to buy some more. We bought tools as we went along too, and because we have always reverenced good tools most of them are still good and will give us years more of use.

Many people feel that they have no talents along the lines necessary to build a house. They will say that they have never been able to do things with their hands in much the same tone that a young girl states that she can't boil water, if the subject of cooking comes up. The chances are that she could if she wanted to. She will have observed how water is obtained from the faucet and that it must be put in some kind of a vessel and heat applied to the bottom of it. In the same way people who have reached a certain age and have lived in houses for some time will know a great deal more about them, or how they personally feel they should be, than they might, at first, think.

Just what they can do will not be known until they try, and if they build something for themselves, by themselves, who is to criticize?

Naturally there will be obstacles and discouragements. Is anything very important ever done without them? The fact remains that overcoming obstacles and discouragements is still one of the most satisfying things that we, as intelligent beings, do.

Speaking of discouragements, don't expect your favorite lumberman to share an enthusiasm for adobe. As purchasing agent of our building materials, I have talked to many of them and find that a lumberman's dream house is always a bungalow built of some rare, imported wood, always hard to get. Although he has no lumber for sale, or at most only a few green boards, a lumberman is not likely to cheer you on your way to building with adobe. Disparagements will come from other directions, too. I think this is because Americans are too close to the pioneer stage to think much of earth as a building medium. My grandmother, were she alive, wouldn't think much of it for she would remember hanging the sheets from her hope chest on the walls of a dug-out in Oklahoma while grandfather built a decent frame house on the land he won in the land lottery. A carpenter by trade, it is likely that he too would think his granddaughter crazy to want a mud house.

People have stopped asking us if we thought our house would stand through a winter as it has obviously stood through several, but we remember one evening after a long, full day of bricklaying when a neighbor asked in all seriousness if we thought it would really stand up. Tired as he was, Paul summoned the patience to answer that he did.

Even if we did get tired at times we took pride in doing every part of our house ourselves, but we needn't have done it that way. Professional help could have been had on any phase of it—the engineering, planning, plumbing, wiring, or carpentering. In a sense we did have such help for we read a great deal on these subjects, material written by experienced men, and we observed their work at every opportunity. If any part of your building seems beyond your abilities, physical or mental, pack up your problems and take them to an experienced person. In many communities it will be possible for you to hire a plumber, an electrician, or a carpenter and act as his "helper." Even a brief apprenticeship of this kind should enable you to continue with much of the work by yourself. The cost of professional services would be reduced in this way in any event.

Once started, you will find that there is a whole world of information to be had for little or nothing. Current magazines, books, and magazine files are at the public libraries; bulletins published by federal and state agencies are available to all. Large commercial associations and mail-order companies publish many booklets and leaflets concerning the use of their products, and these cost nothing but the postage to mail the request.

It may be that all you want or hope to gain by building your own house is the house itself. The by-products of this activity may, however, amaze you. Undertaken by all the members of the family and the family

*The carved mantel decoration and the copper firescreen are but two examples
of hobbies which we acquired while housebuilding.*

friends, it can lead to a stronger family unit and deepened friendships as well as other values which might be termed spiritual. There will be material advantages as weil. You may, within your own family, have artists or craftsmen as yet unaware of their bent. A career might be born as the house is built! A hobby or two is bound to be.

For one reason or another, an adobe house seems able to absorb quantities of handmade decoration without looking ornate, especially when the decoration is a part of the building. It may be that the reason for this lies in the fundamental simplicity that adobe construction demands or because of the quiet strength of the material. Whatever the cause, it would seem impossible to upset the architectural equilibrium of the adobe.

Carving, as an example, decorates our doors, window and door frames, the mantel strip over the fireplace, the beams overhead, and so on. Nearly every piece of furniture we have built for the house shows the marks of my chisels, yet the house is far from being reminiscent of a Swiss woodcarver's cottage.

I had never given woodcarving a thought until Paul brought Herbert Faulkner's *Woodcarving as a Hobby* (Harper & Brothers) home one day and suggested I do some carving for the house. I gathered a few tools and practiced on an old board, cutting my fingers a time or two until I was ready to start on my first project: one button. My second project was a large oak chest, Spanish in feeling and covered with quite intricate designs. Since then I have stopped at nothing in the way of woodcarving and have found it thoroughly satisfying as a means of artistic expression. It has also been a satisfaction to see pictures of much of my work published.

In his book on carving as a hobby, Mr. Faulkner with intent to encourage says that anyone who can sharpen a pencil can carve. This could have discouraged me in the very beginning as I was practically notorious for my horrible pencil-sharpening. Paul swore I did it with my teeth and is still promising to buy me a really good pencil sharpener because I still can't sharpen a pencil unless I use woodcarving tools! I can carve though and so can anyone else who wants to.

Our interest in working with metals such as copper, tin, and iron has had scope in fashioning our own lighting fixtures and much of our hardware. Using mostly scraps and salvaged metal we made a number of lamps and lanterns for porch, yard, and patio and for the interior lights.

Diane took over the tile-setting when we first decided to face our window sills with decorative tile, and she added tile-setting and making tile mosaic to her growing list of hobbies.

Having a hobby, particularly making something, no matter what, has come to be considered the best medicine for everything from boredom to a diseased mind, to say nothing of being the best way to develop the personality. Personality disorders and even physical handicaps are no doubt alleviated by an absorbing interest outside the self, but these are not the reasons we urge you to make your own hobby a part of your house. Our reasons have nothing to do with keeping you out of institutions for the mentally defective. We only hope that you will find the sheer pleasure to be had by including the extensions of the family's personality in your house.

There is a lot of fun in building your own house on week ends. Sunday afternoons that so often bog down in boredom will not be your lot if you are working on your house and the heavy week-end meals so reluctantly digested when turning the pages of a Sunday paper can be eaten with good conscience if there is hard work to be done afterward. Sun tans are acquired as readily while shingling a roof as on a beach— so are sunburns! While speaking of the healthy advantages to be had in building your own house it might be appropriate to mention that accidents can happen because of inexperience, so be careful. Don't overdo until you know what you can do without undue strain. It will do you no harm to get tired if the day's fatigue vanishes after one night's rest. It is best to take it easy until you know just how much building activity makes a day's work for you.

The many different phases of the work will be better understood if they are worked out one at a time too. Solving one problem will give you knowledge that will make the next one simpler; it isn't necessary to know everything there is to know about any part of the building to make a start. Take the first step and go on from there. Read, observe, and ask questions as you go, and with the work done a little at a time and the knowledge gained the same way you can finally have that country home of your own. You can't lose.

Happy building!